LAO TZU'S
TAO TE CHING

Soul Journeying
Commentaries

BOOK COVER SYMBOLISM
Purple • Spiritual Integrity
White • Pure/Clearing/Liberating Energy

LAO TZU'S
TAO TE CHING

Soul Journeying
Commentaries

道 德 經

A Sojourning Pilgrim's Rendering

of

81 Spirit Soul Passages

Raymond Bart Vespe

REGENT PRESS
Berkeley, California

Paperback
ISBN 13: 978-1-58790-429-5
ISBN 10: 1-58790-429-2

E-book:
ISBN 13: 978-1-58790-430-1
ISBN 10: 1-58790-430-6

Library of Congress Control Number: 2017964741

Manufactured in the United States of America

REGENT PRESS
www.regentpress.net
regentpress@mindspring.com

CONTENTS

DEDICATION

For my three sons-in-law, Jeremy Wilson, Shachar Tassa and Ashley Lewin for loving, caring for, protecting, providing for, supporting, encouraging, fostering and enjoying Soul-journeying with my three daughters; Laura Anne, Cheryl Jean and Arianna Selene with whom they generously and gratefully brought my seven grandchildren Grant and Shannon Wilson; Ilanit, Liana, and Oren Tassa; and Avery and Arlen Lewin into this human world and our family during my lifetime.

For my two former wives, Carla and Maia, who co-conceived, birthed and co-parented our daughters and who are continuing to share the beauty of their Spirit and Souls and the joys of grandparenting their children.

For my grandchildren. May you always remember the blessed gift of human life, fully identify with your precious indwelling Spirit and Human Soul, gratefully treasure each new moment of conscious awareness and quietly illuminate your surroundings with the radiant presence of your joyful being. May the fires of your Spirit and Human Soul never dim or cool and may they light and warm every human being whom you meet throughout your life journeying. May you and your generation contribute wholeheartedly to co-creating a more Spiritual, Soulful, sustainable and habitable Human World and Community. It only takes a few real, true, wise, loving and caring Human Beings to awaken many and to transform our needful and waiting world.

ACKNOWLEDGEMENTS

Of all my Spirit-guides and Soul-companions in the Spiritual traditions of Hinduism, Vedanta, Yoga, Tantra and Kashmir Shaivism; Theravada, Mahayana, Vajrayana, Ekayana, Nichiren, Ch'an and Zen Buddhism; Sufism; Taoism; Christian Mysticism and Indigenous Peoples. You have my most profound gratitude for sharing the pilgrimaging to, and the sojourning in, the Sacred places of our awakened and illuminated Human Heart, Minds, Souls, Spirit, Being and Living.

Of Deng Ming-Dao for his numerous dedicated, inspiring and illustrative publications and presentations in the Way and ways of Chinese Taoist being and living and for enlightening me about the nature of Spirit and the Human Soul as understood in Chinese native culture and as cultivated in Chinese Taoist practice.

And, once again, grateful appreciation of my youngest daughter, Arianna Selene Lewin, and my son-in-law, Ashley Evan Lewin, for their ongoing interest, encouragement, support and assistance in word processing the manuscript; and of Mark Weiman of Regent Press for his continuing enthusiasm, competency and proficiency in formatting and publishing the book.

Thank you, one and all, from the center of my Being, the bottom of my Heart, the depth of my Soul and the vast spaciousness of Spirit.

LAO   TZU

老   子

OLD	BOY
AGED	CHILD
EXPERIENCED	SON
ESTABLISHED	GENTLEMAN
WELL-COOKED	PHILOSOPHER
VENERABLE	MASTER

THE OLD BOY/PHILOSOPHER/MASTER.
TERMS OF GREAT HONOR/DEEP RESPECT/HIGH REGARD
FOR LAO TZU, THE PURPORTED AUTHOR OF THE
TAO TE CHING TEXT.[1]

PROLOGUE

WISE YOUNG SOUL	'But just see the radiant beauty of all of this. It's everywhere!'
WISE OLD SOUL	'Yes, my dear friend. Real it is. Spirit is everywhere but only a few of us have been educated about it or awakened to its reality.'
WISE YOUNG SOUL	'But just feel the vital energy of all of this. It's in everything!'
WISE OLD SOUL	'Yes, my dear friend. True it is. Spirit is in everything as its innermost, deepest, centermost, truest and utmost nature and Soul but only a few of us are aware of it or attentive to its truth.'
WISE YOUNG SOUL	'But there is so much life and so many human beings on Earth. It's so sad!'
WISE OLD SOUL	'Yes, my dear friend. Sad it is. If more of us accepted, cherished and nourished life as a precious gift, Sacred blessing and rare opportunity and related to each other as Spirit and Human Souls; our lives and our world would be very different. There would be far less distrust, poverty, hunger, abuse, violence, conflict, war, killing and misery. There would be far more faith, abundance, fulfillment, caring, sharing, harmony, peace, loving and joy.'
WISE YOUNG SOUL	'Now I'm really very sad!'
WISE OLD SOUL	'Yes, my dear friend. So am I. Perhaps you and human beings like you will be able to make a difference and Soulfully co-create a more sustainable life and habitable world.'
WISE YOUNG SOUL	'I truly hope so. I will try my hardest and will do my best for as long as I live!'

WISE OLD SOUL 'Your wholehearted devotion and commitment are worthy of my greatest honor and deepest respect. I will support and assist you; without reservation, qualification or condition; in any and every way that I can throughout the lifetime that I have remaining.'

WISE YOUNG SOUL 'Thank you so much! I'm so happy that we met each other along the way. I love you!'

WISE OLD SOUL 'And thank you so much too! Our meeting means the world to me. And, my dear newly found Spiritual friend, I too, love you!'

INTRODUCTION

Text and Authorship

The *Tao Te Ching* is a beautiful collection of wisdom sayings originating in ancient China approximately two-thousand five-hundred years ago. Its purported author, Lao Tzu/Old Boy/Philosopher/Master, is a 6th Century BCE legendary figure who may or may not have existed and the text may be a compilation of the oral wisdom teachings of many like-hearted sages.

These teachings are essentially advisings by wise sages to feudal rulers about how to order their kingdoms, govern their people and live their lives at a time in Chinese history; the Spring/Ch'ua and Autumn/Ch'iu period (c. 770-475 BCE), of great socio-political division, upheaval and disintegration prior to the Warring States/Chan Kuo period (c. 475-221 BCE), one of bloody internecine warfare between feudal states vying for hegemony.

The *Tao Te Ching* is the principal text of the ancient Chinese philosophical/Spiritual tradition of Taoism and reportedly is the second most translated book in world literature next only to the Holy Bible. Over the some two-thousand five-hundred years, there have been hundreds of translations and commentaries made by dedicated human beings in the fields of politics, martial arts, medicine, philosophy, religion, alchemy and yoga.

The wisdom contained in the *Tao Te Ching* is so essential, universal and timeless that it is perennially adaptable and applicable to, and relevant for, each new age in a wide variety of differing cultures. The wisdom sayings of the *Tao Te Ching* are as meaningful today in the modern West as they were long ago in the Far East and are master keys that are valuable for, and helpful in, acknowledging the Sacredness of Human Being and the process of becoming a Spiritual, Soulful and wise human being;

of living an awakened, conscious and fulfilling human life and of co-creating and sharing a harmonious human world with fellow Spiritual, Soul-journeying and Wayfaring companions.

Most translations of the *Tao Te Ching* are made from the received text first translated and commentaried upon by Wang Pi (c. 226-249 CE). However, two other documents antedating this text are two silk manuscripts (dated c. 168-206 BCE) excavated at Mawangdui in 1973 (with the order of the text reversed to *Te Tao Ching*) and a partial text reassembled from unbundled bamboo slips (dated c. 300 BCE) excavated at Goudian in 1993.

The legend of Lao Tzu begins with his birth sometime during the 6th Century BCE in the feudal State of Ch'u (c. 740-330 BCE) in Southern China. One part of the legend says that he is born white-haired and long-eared; signs of wisdom, enlightenment and longevity. He is an archivist in the court of the Later/ Eastern Chou Dynasty (c. 770-221 BCE), becomes disheartened by the pervasive socio-political intrigues during the Spring and Autumn period, mounts an ox and commences to leave China heading westward toward India, Tibet and the Gobi Desert.

At Han Ku Kuan, the Gobi Desert valley frontier mountain pass, Lao Tzu is stopped by Kuan Yin Hsi, keeper of the pass, who recognizes his sagehood and makes his passage contingent upon transmitting the essence of his wisdom. Lao Tzu complies and approximately five-thousand Chinese characters are inked on bamboo slips later bundled and tied together by Kuan Yin Hsi. Following this, Lao Tzu again mounts his ox and proceeds westward to the Kun-Lun mountains, the axis of the world and abode of immortal beings. The sayings become known as *The Lao Tzu/Book of Lao Tzu*, after his authorship, and later on are titled the *Tao Te Ching* as we know it today.

Regardless of the indefinite determination and veracity of the *Tao Te Ching's* authorship, we do have an actual document containing quintessential wisdom which has been, and is, a perennial classic of ancient Chinese Taoist philosophy, Spirituality and Way of being and living. And the legend of Lao Tzu is a beautiful metaphor for the human experience of developing wisdom; disengaging from socio-cultural, interpersonal and/or intrapsychic conflict; transmitting this wisdom for the benefit of fellow human beings and ultimately transitioning through elevated frontier passageways to timeless realms.

Experiential Concepts

The experiential concepts found embedded throughout the *Tao Te Ching* are essentially those of the philosophical/Spiritual tradition of ancient Chinese Taoism as follows:

Wu Chi	The nonmaterial/nonphysical/non-ultimate/No-thingness of Tao's void.
Yuan Ch'i	Primordial/undifferentiated/originating/creating energy of Tao.
Tao	Ultimate Reality/All That Is/As It Is/Everywhere At Once/Here And Now.
Te	The unique individualizing/efficacious power/creative Virtuosity of our authenticity/inner truth/integrity/genius/excellence/inborn Tao-nature.
Ch'i	The all-pervading/animating/nourishing/sustaining vital energy/life force of Tao present and circulating everywhere in our human body/world/cosmos/universe.
Yin/Yang Ch'i	The bipolar/complementary/interdependent/alternating/reciprocating/reversing dynamics of Tao's regulating.
Wu Wei Ch'i	The frictionless/effortless/seamless/flowing/circulating/cycling/returning kinetics of Tao's operating.
Tzu Jan	the natural/free/spontaneous presencing

of any/all of the phenomena of our human existing/consciousness/awareness/experiencing.

Wan Wu   the infinite variety/totality of diverse beings/phenomena/objects/things in the phenomenological world of our human consciousness/awareness/existence/experience.

Sheng Jen   Sacred/wise human beings who are embodying/assimilating/personifying/enacting/identifying with/*as* Tao and its characteristics/qualities/operations/activities.

T'ien Ti   the integral Heavenly/celestial and the Earthly/terrestrial dimensions and Tao-natures of our human being/existing/consciousness/experiencing.

Shen Shen   the integral embodied Spirit/body-Spirit and the inSpirited body/Spirit-body in the lower/belly and upper/head energy centers/elixir fields/Tan T'iens of our human body.

Hsin   the Heart-Mind middle energy center of our body and Human Being as the integrative harmonizing center of Heaven-Earth (Nature), body-Spirit/Spirit-body and the lower/belly-upper/head energy centers of our body and human being; the central Heart, Pivot and Axis of Tao.

Hun P'o   the integral Heavenly/Spiritual and the Earthly/physical twin Souls of our Human Being/Deeper and Higher Self.

The following is a selected listing of some roughly categorized words, terms and concepts and the approximate frequency ranges of their individual occurrence in the *Tao Te Ching* text.

No/Not-/Non-/Un-/Without
= *total over 250 x.*

Nothingness/Non-Being/Non-Doing
= *each between 100-300 x.*

Being/Having/Oneness/Self/Heaven/Lowness/Greatness/Human Being
= *each between 80-100 x.*

Life/Wholeness/Te/Knowing/Goodness/Speaking/Tao
= *each between 40-80 x.*

Softness/Darkness/Returning/Completeness/Sacredness/Ruling/People/Things/Clearness/Stillness
= *each between 30-40 x.*

Using/Sufficiency/Origin/Richness/Allness/Name/Happiness/Desiring
= *each between 20-30 x.*

Heart-Mind/Simplicity/Trueness/Spirit/Soul/Smallness/Love/Following/Death/Earth
= *each between 10-20 x.*

Breath/Body/Vastness/Centeredness/Emptiness/Openness/Water/Mother/Child/Valley/Wheel/Yin-Yang
= *each under 10x.*

The above listings clearly and unequivocally identify the Chinese Taoist tradition and *Tao Te Ching* wisdom as a vital Spiritual and Soulful *via negativa* of great Human significance, relevance and importance.

Metaphors and Meditations

The wisdom sayings of the *Tao Te Ching* can be considered from two complementary perspectives, i.e., literally, outwardly and exoterically and metaphorically, inwardly and esoterically as follows:

EXOTERIC	ESOTERIC
The State/country	Tao/Ultimate/NondualReality/Tao-State
Rulers/leaders	Our main/executive ego-identity/'I'
People/subjects	Our many different egos/'me's
The empire/kingdom	Our life as a whole
Sages/wise human beings	Our Deeper/Higher Self/Tao-Self
The 10,000 things	Our many diverse experiential phenomena
Ruling/governing	Our Self-regulating

So, in the outer exoteric theater of the *Tao Te Ching*, the cast of characters is unnamed rulers and leaders who are being advised by wise and fully developed human beings on ways of existing and ways of governing their kingdoms, ordering their people and attaining a unified country. And, in the inner esoteric theater of the *Tao Te Ching*, the cast of characters is our specific named main and executive egos who are being advised by our Deeper and Higher Tao-Selves on ways of Being and ways of regulating our lives as a whole, harmonizng our many subordinate egos and returning to a Tao-State of Integral/Nondual Reality.

Though not explicitly focused on, understanding and experiencing the material contained in this rendition of the *Tao Te Ching* metaphorically makes it extremely useful for supporting, assisting, facilitating and guiding self-awakening, self-regulating, self-developing, self-transforming and self-fulfilling.

The terms and concepts found in the *Tao Te Ching* are not abstract and intellectual but are, instead, actual realities that can be directly, concretely and immediately experienced in classic meditative states of visualization, concentration, contemplation, reflection and absorption. You are invited and encouraged to openly receive, reflect upon, respond to and reside in the material in a quiet and comfortable setting; with slow, deep and full breathing and in a calm and relaxed state of being.

Rendition and Title

The present work is technically not a translation of the *Tao Te Ching* but, rather, a rendition and, more specifically, the literary equivalent of a jazz rendition characterized by some occasional solo improvised flights that depart from a musical composition as originally scored. This rendition falls somewhere between the nearly accurate and sometimes sterile literal translations of academic sinologists and the nearly unrecognizable and sometimes juvenile fanciful adaptations of idiosyncratic apologists.

Much has been explicated concerning the identity of Spiritual Reality and the nature of the Human Soul as found in world mythologies, religions and philosophies; Spiritual, mystical, arcane, occult and esoteric traditions; primitive, indigenous and shamanic cultures and cosmological, theological, ontological, anthropological, sociological, psychological, parapsychological and ecological disciplines; as well as being present in the awakened and enlightened consciousness, experiencing and understanding of collective humanity.

This work assumes the essential reality of Spirit and the existential actuality of our Human Soul but does not attempt to define either. As was thought to be so in times past, it is now known that the existence of our Human Soul cannot be proven by the post-mortem weighing of human bodies or be physically seated in the pineal gland of human brains.

However, the reality of Spirit and the actuality of our Human Soul are evidenced in the existence of incarnated Avatars, reincarnated Bodhisattvas and Lamas and by human beings, for example, remembering past lives and choosing parents and those undergoing pre-natal, out-of-body, near-death and post-mortem experiences and those being visited by, contacting and communicating with Spirits and Souls of the deceased.

The reality and actuality of Spirit and our Human Soul also have been evidenced by/in human beings who have 'experienced' preternatural, supernatural, paranormal and psychic powers and phenomena in non-ordinary and 'altered' states of conscious-ness during, for example, shamanic journeys and vision quests; ecstatic trance drumming, chanting and dancing; ritual sacri-ficing, offering and praying; yogic, meditative and breathing practices; clairvoyant, clairaudient, clairsentient, intuitve and dream states; psychedelic and psychotropic sessions, hypnotic age regressions and rebirthing, fasting and sensory deprivation et al that involve inducing and facilitating a transcending of the ordinary space-time limitations of our physical body, conceptual mind, ego-self and mundane existence.

In this work, our Human Soul is purely and simply consid-ered as being the integration of our human embodying of Spirit and the inSpiriting of our human body. Our Human Soul is an integral body-Spirit and a Spirit-body. Any further consideration as to its actual reality, nature, qualities, characteristics, attributes and activities rests with the undeniable and unequivocal Soulful experiences of human beings who are embodying, personifying, enacting and identifying themselves *as* a Human Soul.

The main focus in this rendition of the *Tao Te Ching* is on the identity of Tao and Spirit, Te and Human Soul and Ch'i as the Energy of Spirit and Soul. Various descriptions of the nature, qualities, characteristics, attributes and activities of Spirit and our Human Soul are considered as being synonymous with descriptions of those of Tao and Te found in Lao Tzu's *Tao Te Ching*. The entire text can be considered as an exposition of var-ious passages that our Human Soul makes and takes in its ener-gized journeying throughout our human life course, life cycle and life span from physical incarnation to Spiritual awakening, from ego-identification to Spirit-identification.

However, the synonymous descriptions and identifications made for this rendition are very general and oversimplified ones that only correlate modern Chinese and English language dictionary definitions of Spirit, Soul and Energy. They do not refer to or include the specific Chinese Taoist Spiritual, philosophical and cultural understandings, articulations and expositions of the nature, qualities, characteristics, attributes and activities of Spirit, Human Soul and Energy which are beyond the limited scope of this rendition and its author's competence.

In this rendition, the title of the *Tao Te Ching*, usually translated as the *Tao/Way Virtue/Power Classic*, is instead rendered as *Spirit Soul Passages*. Tao is the Supreme/Ultimate Reality that equates closely with the nature, qualities, characteristics, attributes and activities of Spirit. Te is the uniquely individualized embodiment and personification of, and identification with/ *as*, Tao, our inborn Tao-nature, and equates closely with the nature, qualities, characteristics, attributes and activities of our Human Soul; our innermost, deepest, centermost, truest and utmost Spirit-nature.

Ching is translated etymologically as the experiencing of the passages of deep underground watercourses and lengthwise loom threadings and equates closely with the nature, qualities, characteristics, attributes and activities of the journeying of our Human Soul and the many transformative passages constituting Soul-work, Soul-making, Soul-journeying and the 'enSouling' process throughout the life course, life cycle and life span of our human being and becoming.

The Sacred/Holy/saintly/sagely/wise human beings/Sheng Jen referred to throughout the *Tao Te Ching* are here rendered as Tao/Spirit-identified human beings who are living a Spirit-grounded, focused, centered and Soulful life. Tao/Spirit-identifying human beings are the quintessential awakened embodying, realizing, personifiying, actualizing and enacting of Tao/Spirit and Te/Human Soul and their spontaneously presencing, dynamically transforming and kinetic unfolding in our world of fellow human beings; in our existing, consciousness, awareness, experiencing, interrelating and living and in the lifelong journeying of our Human Soul as an integral embodied/incorporated body-Spirit and an inSpirited/animated Spirit-body.

Subtitle and Commentary

The subtitle of this rendition reflects the author's identifying as a sojourning pilgrim. The dictionary definition of 'pilgrimage' is that of 'the journey of a pilgrim' and 'the course of life on earth'. A 'pilgrim' is 'one who journeys/travels in foreign lands, usually as a devotee, to a shrine/Sacred place/location'. 'Sojourn' is 'to stay/lodge/reside/abide/dwell briefly/momentarily/temporarily/transiently as one who is passing through somewhere'.

The wording of the subtitle is carefully chosen to metaphorically represent 1) the journey of our Human Soul from the strange land of the ego to the Sacred abode of Spirit, 2) our Human Soul's temporary stay during the course of its human being and living on Earth and 3) the passages of our Human Soul on its journeying/traveling/wayfaring as they involve exploring; a sense of ad-venture/advent-ure through unmapped pristine wilderness frontiers and discovering the Reality of Spirit present at/in/as Sacred sites, holy places, consecrated lands, hallowed grounds, energy centers and power spots.[2]

Our Human Soul undergoes and experiences many transformative passages in its journeying through life and, as journeying Souls and Spirit-identifying human beings, we are constantly, continually and continuously passaging from, to and between various states of being, consciousness and existing. Passages are 'roads/paths/ways/courses/channels from one place/situation/condition to another.' Traveling/journeying/wayfaring/sojourning are names for the passaging process in Soul-work, Soul-making and enSouling; the endowing and imbuing of our Human Being with/*as* a Human Soul, an embodied Spirit and an inSpirited body.

In this rendition of *Spirit Soul Passages*, each one of the 81 transformative passages of our Human Soul is followed by a brief summary explication of its essential message and the relevant qualities, characteristics, attributes and/or activities of Spirit-identifying Human Beings. This is followed by a 'commentary' that is a meditative inquiry in the form of a series of contemplative questions addressed to us as journeying Human Souls. The questions relate to the focus, conduct and potential ways of human being and living that are involved in and/or result from Soul-work, Soul-making, the enSouling process and Soul-journeying throughout our human life course, life cycle and life span.

Completing this Spirit/Soul-grounded, focused and centered rendition of, and commentary upon, Lao Tzu's *Tao Te Ching* has been an extremely meaningful, integrating, gratifying, rewarding, enjoyable and heartwarming personal experience in my own Soul-work, Soul-making, enSouling and Soul-journeying. If this material is of some, or any, interest, value, inspiration, encouragement, support, assistance, guidance and benefit for you in awakening to, discovering, experiencing, understanding and sharing the reality and actualities of your own enSouling and the Soul-passaging of your own Spiritual wayfaring and sojourning pilgrimage; I am infinitely pleased and eternally grateful.

Raymond Bart Vespe
Santa Rosa, California
Winter Solstice, 2017

CH'I

氣

BREATH
AIR/STEAM/GAS/VAPOR/ETHER/SMOKE
VITAL ENERGY/LIFE FORCE/COSMIC SPIRIT

LIFE-CONSTITUTING/PERVADING/SUSTAINING
ANIMATING/ACTIVATING/VITALIZING/NOURISHING
COSMIC ORDER/NATURAL LAWS/WORLD PROCESS
UBIQUITOUS/EVER-PRESENT/EVER-CIRCULATING
PRIMORDIAL/NON-MATERIAL/UNDIFFERENTIATED
ACQUIRED/MATERIAL/DIFFERENTIATED
ENDOWED/PRESERVED/CULTIVATED/CONSERVED
MANNER/TEMPER/DISPOSITION/BEARING/STYLE
2 PRINCIPLES (YIN/YANG)
YIN/YANG CH'I/WU WEI CH'I

SYNONYMOUS WITH TRANSCENDENT/IMMANENT TAO

YIN/YANG CH'I DYNAMICS

GENERATING/ORIGINATING
FORMING/TRANSFORMING
ALTERNATING/RECIPROCATING
COMPENSATING/EQUALIZING
BALANCING/CENTERING
VOIDING/REVERSING

WU WEI CH'I KINETICS

ESSENTIAL/NECESSARY
APPROPRIATE/SUITABLE
FLOWING/CIRCULATING
SEAMLESS/CONTINUOUS
FRICTIONLESS/EFFORTLESS
CYCLING/RETURNING

Ch'i as Human Energy

Tao is often identified as, and equated with, Ch'i, the universal and pervasive animating, activating, nourishing and sustaining vital energy, life force and creative principle/*elan vital* present, freely flowing, circulating and evolving in and throughout the universe, cosmos, natural world, living beings and our human body.

The Chinese character for Ch'i is variously translated as breath, air, steam, vapor, ether, gas, smoke, life-giving principle, vital energy, life force, spirit, bearing, manner, demeanor, temperment, style and the Two Principles (Yin and Yang).

Ch'i is all-pervading and all-constituting and is both non-material-material, Spiritual-physical and energy-matter. It is formless, invisible and intangible energy with the potential to condense, congeal and coagulate and materialize form. Much like electrical energy, Ch'i energy is known to exist by virtue of the effects that it produces in the physical world, beings and things.

Ch'i energy is inherent in the originating, forming, manifesting and transforming of all natural phenomena. Life forms are the gathering of Ch'i energy; the living process is its constant, continuous and continual flowing, circulating and transforming and death is its dispersing, dissipating and ceasing.

Ch'i energy can be identified with the following experiential concepts found in the philosophical/Spiritual tradition of ancient Chinese Taoism:

Wu Ch'i	No-thingness/nonmaterial/sourcing energy of the Void.
Yuan Ch'i	Primordial/undifferentiated/creating energy of the Origin.
Tao Ch'i	Absolutizing/totalizing/all-pervading energy of Ultimate Reality.
Ch'i	Animating/activating/vitalizing/sustaining energy of the Life Force.
Te Ch'i	Differentiating/individualizing/potentiating energy of Virtuosity.
Yin/Yang Ch'i	Bipolar/alternating/reversing energies of Shaded/Sunny Dynamics.
Wu Wei Ch'i	Flowing/circulating/returning energies of Non-Doing Kinetics.
Sheng Jen Ch'i	Embodied/personified/Sacralized energy of Human Being.
Tzu Jan Ch'i	Naturally presencing/manifesting/appearing energy of Self-So-ness.
Wan Wu Ch'i	Objectified/differentiated/diversified energy of the Myriad Things.
T'ien Ti Ch'i	Celestial/terrestrial/universal/cosmic energies of Heaven-Earth.
Shen Shen Ch'i	Physical/embodied/Spiritual/inSpirited energies of Body-Spirit/Spirit-Body
Hsin Ch'i	Centralized/integrated/harmonized energy of Heart-Mind.
Hun P'o Ch'i	Coalescing/evanescing energies of Spiritual-Physical Twin Souls.

Ch'i energy is both primordial and acquired and respectively equates with the attributes, characteristics, qualities and activities of Tao and Te as follows:

Tao Ch'i	*Te Ch'i*
Primordial/prenatal	Acquired/postnatal
Nonmaterial/nonphysical	Material/physical
Undifferentiated/formless	Individualized/formed
Transcendent potentiality	Immanent actuality
Cosmic energy/spirit	Vital energy/fluid
Light force/illumination	Life force/animation
Radiant luminosity	Potent vitality
Primal aura/atmosphere	Halo/corona/nimbus
Emanating/radiating	Gathering/condensing
Ultimate Reality	Intimate Virtuosity
Spirit/L. *animus*	Soul/L. *anima*
Spirit of Tao	Body of Tao
Spiritual/endowed	Soulful/cultivated
Needs preserving	Needs reserving
Needs safeguarding	Needs conserving

Primordial Ch'i energy is originally an undifferentiated chaos rooted in the empty void space of Non-Being, the Nonultimate/ Wu Chi. It differentiates into Great Yang/Heaven/Yang Ch'i and Great Yin/Earth/Yin Ch'i and our Spiritual Soul/Hun and physical Soul/P'o. Their integration with Wu Chi forms the Supreme Ultimate/T'ai Chi which generates all of the myriad diverse beings and things in the universe, natural world and human existence and experience along with their endless flux, changing and transforming.

The constant, continuous and continual bipolar alternating, reciprocating and reversing of Yin/Yang Ch'i energies and their Wu Wei Ch'i seamless flowing, circulating and returning activities are the dynamic-kinetic operations of Tao and the efficacious power of its Virtuosity, Te. The following are some attributes, characteristics, qualities and activities of Yin Ch'i/Yang Ch'i and Wu Wei Ch'i:

Yin Ch'i	*Yang Ch'i*	*Wu Wei Ch'i*
Passive/receptive	Active/creative	No-/not-/non-doing
Magnetic/attracting	Dynamic/expressing	No 'thing'-doing
Contracting/condensing	Expanding/radiating	No-thing 'doing'
Centripetal/afferent	Centrifugal/efferent	Tao-sourced activity
Yielding/receptive	Firm/assertive	Flowing/coursing
Retreating/retrogressing	Advancing/progressing	Circulating/cycling
Still/internal/central	Moving/external/peripheral	Rotating/revolving
Inner depth/hidden	Outer surface/manifest	Frictionless
Shaded/dark/dim	Sunny/light/bright	Effortless
Cold/watery/wet/soft	Hot/fiery/dry/hard	Seamless
Cloudy/heavy/closed	Clear/light/open	Continuous
Below/behind/within	Above/ahead/around	Natural activity
Negative/empty	Positive/full	Unforced/unmanipulated
Earthly/material	Heavenly/Spiritual	Purposeless/goalless
Ground/support	Sky/canopy	Creative actions
Dusk/night/lunar/winter	Dawn/day/solar/summer	Original actions
Feminine principle in Nature	Masculine principle in Nature	Essential actions
Creatrix/Mother/queen	Creator/Father/king	Necessary actions
Valleys/canyons/caverns	Mountains/hills/mounds	Appropriate actions
Ebbing/waning/troughing	Flowing/waxing/peaking	Suitable actions
Physical Soul/P'o	Spiritual Soul/Hun	Harmonious actions
Embodied Spirit/body-Spirit	InSpirited body/Spirit-body	Spontaneity/serendipity

Yin/Yang Ch'i dynamics are regulated by the Law of Reversal such that when one pole of a given nondual bipolar interdependent relationship reaches its maximum point; it alternates, reciprocates, counterbalances, compensates, voids itself and reverses to its complementary pole. Wu Wei Ch'i kinetics are governed by the Law of Return such that the non-linear energy flows, circulates, rotates, revolves, cycles and returns to its original source. A useful illustrative analogy for the dynamic-kinetic operating of these energies is that of a non-digital clock, where the tic-toc is the alternating and reversing Yin/Yang dynamic and the rotating hands are the cycling and returning Wu Wei kinetic.

Ch'i energy is cultivated and compounded by reserving the physical energy of generative essence/Ching, conserving the vital energies of Yin/Yang Ch'i and Wu Wei Ch'i and preserving the Spiritual energy/Shen of Primordial Ch'i and of alchemically refining and transmuting Ching into the vitality of Ch'i energy and Ch'i into the reality of Spirit/Shen. This is accomplished in yogic practices that utilize the three lower/belly, middle/heart and upper/head energy centers or elixir fields/Tan T'iens and the macrocosmic and microcosmic orbits or energy pathways in our human body.

T'ai Chi Ch'uan/Supreme Ultimate Boxing and Ch'i Kung/Energy Work are two Chinese Taoist moving meditation practices that promote physical, emotional, mental, social and Spiritual health and well-being through the grounding, centering, flowing, circulating, balancing, integrating, harmonizing and optimizing of Ch'i energy. In Chinese medical practice, acupuncture, acupressure and moxibustion treatments make use of specific energy points and meridians in the human body to stimulate, unblock, compensate and counterbalance Yin/Yang and Wu Wei Ch'i energies. Also, Chinese herbal medicines and preparations are similarly used to activate, mobilize, circulate, balance and harmonize Ch'i energy in the treatment of health issues. Furthermore, the art of Chinese geomancy/Feng/Shui (Wind/Water) makes use of Ch'i energy fields and currents of the earth and the structural qualities and environmental placements of objects to correct imbalances in and to enhance Ch'i energy.

The vital energy and life force of Ch'i energy are more easily preserved and conserved by not wasting and squandering, leaking and draining, weakening and depleting and/or dispersing and dissipating them by engaging in extraneous and irrelevant, meaningless and useless, pointless and futile, extreme and excessive, inefficient and ineffective, resistant and defensive and/or forced, striving, effortful and conflicted behaviors, relationships, activities and pursuits.

In common parlance, the word 'energy' is used to refer to the vitality of human beings, e.g., our vim, vigor, vivacity, liveliness, verve, pizzazz and panache. Some of us are high energy and others of us are low energy. Someone who is energetic has capacity, stamina, perseverence, endurance and seemingly inexhaustible energy, never running out of energy. Hard work of long duration involves exertion and the expenditure of a great deal of energy. Shopping at crowded malls and waiting in long lines can be enervating and energy draining. We often identify other human beings as having positive and 'good' energy or negative and 'bad' energy 'vibes' which correspondingly influence our own. We can feel activated and potentiated being around vibrantly alive and high energy human beings and deadened and depleted by being around overly needy and chronically depressed human beings. We lend energy and send energy to support, assist and heal human beings. Our physical body is surrounded by an etheric energy body, as reflected in the nature, color and quality of our aura.

Many of us human beings attempt to 'get' energy 'lifts' by consuming coffee and caffeine; energy drinks, shakes and bars; eating chocolate, sugar and carbohydrates or by drinking alcohol for the 'buzz', smoking marijuana or using amphetamines, cocaine and other stimulants and 'uppers' for the 'high' that they may provide. Still others of us seem addicted to the adrenalin rushes, excitation and 'boosts' of prolonged exercise, extreme sports, daredevil activities, dangerous situations, threatening circumstances, conflicted relationships and stressful living.

Human beings with strong Ch'i energy generally live a moderate, frugal and economical and frictionless, harmonious and effortless life. They are embodying the inner vitality, capacity, potency, efficacy and creativity of the Virtuosity/Te of Tao that are exhibited in their abilities, talents, gifts and genius; that by which their goodness, kindness, beauty, grace and excellence are individually, uniquely, generously, gratefully and happily lived, expressed and shared. Human beings with weak Ch'i energy generally live a powerless, vulnerable and insecure; compromised, struggling and stressful and painful, fearful and miserable life.

Human beings who are robust, vigorous and energetic, vibrant, radiant and charismatic and enthusiastic and passionate are enlivening, invigorating and refreshing and stimulating, empowering and potentiating. They have a deep and full reservoir of strong, freely flowing and fully circulating Ch'i energy.

Human beings who are fatigued, listless and dampened are, to some degree, enervating, exhausting and deadening and have a shallow and nearly empty reserve of weak, depleted, blocked and/or stuck Ch'i energy.

Unfortunately, constantly dealing with, e.g., terminal illness; untreatable disease, chronic physical disability and mental illness; unremitting pain, intractable conditions and refractory health issues; characterological, personality and behavioral disorders; post-traumatic stress disorders; ongoing mental, emotional, physical and sexual abuse and violence; economic poverty, joblessness and homelessness; gender, racial, ethnic, religious, social class and sexual identification discrimination, inequalities and struggles; institutionalization, incarceration and hospitalizations; social isolation and interpersonal conflict; failure, loss and grief; addiction, etc. are realistically and understandably extremely energy debilitating and exhausting for the affected human beings, as well as for their family members, any associates and their caregivers.

TAO

道

ROAD/PATH/WAY
PRINCIPLE/DOCTRINE
REALITY/LOGOS/TRUTH
LAW/ORDER/METHOD
SPEAK/LEAD/GUIDE
THE WAY

MAKING STEP BY STEP HEADWAY ON THE
WAY ONE IS VISIONING AND PROCEEDING.

ABSOLUTE/ESSENTIAL/ONE/ULTIMATE REALITY
CONSTANT/REGULAR/INFINITE/ETERNAL
ORIGIN/SOURCE/DESTINY/FINALITY
TRANSCENDENT/NO-THING
IMMANENT/ALL THINGS
NATURE/HEAVEN-EARTH/UNIVERSE

ALL THAT IS/AS IT IS/EVERYWHERE AT ONCE/HERE/NOW

Tao as Human Spirit

Both Tao and Spirit share the pantheistic-like belief that Tao/ Spirit *is* everything and everything *is* Tao/Spirit and the panentheistic-like belief that Tao/Spirit is *in* everything and everything is *in* Tao/Spirit. Tao and Spirit also share some of the same following attributes, characteristics, qualities and activities:

Ultimate Reality/Great Mystery/Absolute Truth/Essential
   Principle/Logos/Rational Intelligence.
Light/Heaven-Earth/Cosmic Design/Nature/Natural Law/
   Universal Order/Life/World Process.
Everything/All-Being/Existential Totality/Ubiquitous/All That
   Is As It Is Everywhere At Once.
No-Thing/Non-Being/Suprasensory/Transphenomenal/
   Phenomenological Absence.
Non-Material/Non-Physical/Formless/Dimensionless/
   Invisible/Intangible/Transcendent.
Infinite/Eternal/Nondual/Integral/Whole/Complete/Constant/
   Unity/Oneness/Identity.
Omnipresent/Omniscient/Omnipotent/All-Encompassing/
   Embracing/Pervading/Inhering.
Unconditioned/Independent/Unbound/Unlimited/Indivisible/
   Inexhaustible/Infallible.
Origin/Source/Beginning/Agency/Creativity/Destiny/Fate/
   Finality/End/Alpha-Omega.
Animating/Vitalizing/Activating/Enlivening/Motivating/
   Potentiating/Catalyzing Energy.
Bestowing/Blessing/Providential/Influencing/Nourishing/
   Protecting/Guiding/Saving.
Embodied/Personified as Creatrix/Creator/Goddesses/Gods/
   God/Deities/Divinities.[3]
Incarnated/Identified as Supernatural/Superphysical/
   Superhuman/Holy/Sacred Beings.[4]
Present in/as Pure/Supramental/Awakened/Illuminated/
   Enlightened Consciousness.

Greatest/Highest/Fullest/Innermost/Deepest/Centermost/
    Truest/Utmost Human Self.
Often identified as/synonymous with Mind/Psyche/
    Consciousness/Higher Self/Soul.

The principal Chinese character for Spirit/Shen is also translated as: god/diety/divinity/spiritual/divine/transcendent/ supernatural/soul/mind/genius/energy and is etymologically composed of characters that are defined as above/superior/first/ Heaven/reveal/extend/small which collectively denote and connote transcendent, Divine and Spiritual revelation extending to the microcosmic natural and human world.

Another Chinese character for Spirit/Ling is translated as: transcendent/divine/spiritual/soul/intelligence/ingenuity/efficacy/powerful force/subtle substance/the spiritual energy of a being acting upon others and is etymologically composed of characters that are defined as falling rain and interpreted as dancing wizards ritually inducing the descent of rain spirits to the earth below. The combination of several other characters are defined as Great Spirit of Heaven-Earth/Above-Below. Also, there are characters denoting spirits of the Earth, animal spirits and the Valley Spirit, the Mysterious Feminine, Primordial Mother of All-Being.

Finally, another Chinese character/Kuei relating to 'spirit' is defined as: 1) spirits of the dead; 2) departed spirits; 3) disembodied spirits of manes, the deceased who died under strange or violent circumstances or who, for whatever reason, were not properly honored by appropriate ceremonial rituals, offerings, sacrifices or burials and who, except for ancestors, are variously referred to as ghosts, goblins, spectres, apparitions, demons and devils and; 4) diabolical spirits that exert evil influences upon the Earth.

Tao, as Human Spirit, is identified as the real, true, genuine, authentic and essential uniquely embodied inborn nature of human beings. It is the quintessential nature of Heaven and is reflected in luminosity and Spiritual brilliance, numinosity and numenous cosmic power, intuitive wisdom and visionary intelligence and far-reaching healing, transforming, harmonizing and enlightening influences that are mysterious, supernatural and filled with a sense of the presence of Divinity and the Holy that Spiritually appeals to our deeper and higher emotions and aesthetic and refined sensibilities.

Spirit is the life-giving energy that animates, activates, sustains, guides, protects and perfects the living, developing and evolving of human beings and the talent, genius and creativity of virtuoso artists and master artisans. It is the efficacious power of the Virtuosity/Te of Tao residing inwardly in the heart-minds of all human beings. The Human Being of Spirit is a companion and counterpart of Heaven and rests in the harmonious equality, countless blessings and endless joys of Heaven where our Human Spirit and the Spirit of Heaven are one and the same identity.

Again, in common parlance, the qualities and influences of 'spirit' are variously regarded as mysterious and miraculous, supernatural and Divine, nonmaterial and invisible, animating and enlivening, inspiring and uplifting, Sacred and Holy and unequivocal and undeniable. Some of the various meanings of 'spirit' are captured in phrases such as:

Spirit gum (adhesive)
Distilled spirits (alcohol)
Bel esprit (fine minded)
School spirit (loyalty)
Esprit de Corps (honor)
Spirit of the times (ethos)
Holiday spirit (celebratory)

Spirit turpentine (solvent)
Free spirit (independent)
Animal spirit (vivacity)
True spirit (essence)
Good spirits (happy)
High spirited (energetic)
Untamed spirit (wild)

Spirit varnish (coating)
Low spirits (sad)
Poor spirited (zestless)
Mean spirited (nasty)
Spirited away (mysterious)
Disembodied spirit (ghost)
Evil spirit (demonic)

Spirit seance	Spirit rapping	Spirit writing
(invoking)	(presencing)	(communicating)
Great Spirit	Holy Ghost	Holy Spirit
(Sacred)	(religious)	(religious)

Spiritual human beings, while not necessarily religious, are usually believers in divine beings and higher powers; an afterlife and Heavenly realm; goddesses and gods; angels and fairies; divine guardianship, influences, guidance and interventions; ethical principles and moral values and the Sacredness of human beings and all life.

Intimate friends are cherished Spiritual companions; marriage is a Sacred Spiritual union (Greek - *hieros-gamos*); conceiving, birthing and parenting a child is a precious Spiritual blessing and many rites of passage are meaningful Spiritual life events. Spirit is often associated with radiant light and luminosity of some sort, e.g., in the coronas and scintillas of celestial bodies, the halos and nimbuses of religious figures; the icons and artifacts of Spiritual veneration and worship; the auras and sparkling eyes of awakened human beings; the glowing light of beloved lovers; the shining radiance of pregnant women; the contagious effulgence of delighted children. Human Beings of Spirit are experienced as bright, brilliant, radiant, splendid, magnificent, majestic, glorious, charismatic and exquisitely beautiful.

Human beings who are awake, enlightened and Spirit-identified and upright, straightforward and enthusiastic are illuminating, inspiring and uplifting and validating, affirming and sacralizing. They have a solid and abiding identification with/*as* Heavenly, Divine and Human Spirit.[5] Human beings who are godless, faithless and nihilistic are despiriting, disturbing and oppressing and, in some instances, have the separated, alienated and fragmented nature of abandoned, dark, desolate, agitated and/or malevolent spirits.

Human beings who are separated, alienated and isolated from Spirit generally live a restless, hungry and frustrating and seeking, dissatisfying and unfulfilling life. Human beings with a solid Spirit-identification generally live a committed, responsible and accountable and honest, trustworthy and devoted life. They are embodying the inner divinity, integrity, Spirituality, essentiality, constancy and intimacy of the Virtuosity/Te of Tao/Spirit that are evident in their character, refinement and dignity; that by which their gratitude, respectfulness, impartiality, equanimity, humility, patience, generosity and forgiveness are constantly, continuously, continually, faithfully and beneficially expressed and shared.

In sharp contrast, 'spirit' also refers to spirits of the deceased who have 'crossed over' but are somehow troubled, unsettled, unfinished or trapped and can be contacted through mediums and seances. Such disincarnate spirits can be lost or stuck, desire to be reincarnated, may want to enter and to possess a body and displace a Soul and can be malevolent, evil and demonic; taking the forms of ghosts, phantoms, apparitions, spectres and shades that frighten, haunt, taunt, bother, trick and plague human beings and require commands to progress or desist and/or ritual exorcisms to remove them.

In addition to disembodied spirits, there are despirited bodies, e.g., the so-called living dead, zombies or undead vampires. Such beings usually exist in a hell realm characterized by either the terror of being a disembodied spirit or the horror of being a despirited body, caught in a separated, alienated, divided and dissociated state as, to be more poetic, one of either thin vapor fearing the wind or dry flesh longing for rain. Their horror of such 'living' is being a dark body-mass spasm without a Spirit and their terror of such 'dying' is being a dark spirit-vast schism without a body.

TE

徳

VIRTUE
POWER/ENERGY
CHARACTER/EXCELLENCE
RIGHTEOUSNESS
GOODNESS/KINDNESS

**LISTENING/UNDERSTANDING/RELATING UPRIGHTLY/
STRAIGHTFORWARDLY FROM THE REALITY/TRUTH OF ONE'S
HEART-MIND.**

INBORN/INNATE TAO-NATURE
UNIQUE INDIVIDUALITY
INNER TRUTH/INTEGRITY
EFFICACIOUS POTENCY
PRESENCE/IN-FLUENCE
VIRTUOSITY/GENIUS

Te as Human Soul

As Human Soul, Te is the co-existing integration of transcendent and immanent Tao/Spirit and the co-existing integration of Spirit and our human body as a body-Spirit and Spirit-body. Te/Human Soul is embodied and personified Tao/Spirit and is the Virtuosity of our human inborn Tao/Spirit-nature. Te and our Human Soul share some of the same following attributes, characteristics, qualities and activities:

Embodied Tao/Spirit/en-Tao-ed/inSpirited body/incarnation/ animation.

Essence/nonmaterial/nonphysical/non-objective/infinite/ eternal/immortal.

Existence/material/physical/objective/phenomenal/finite/ temporal/mortal.

Nondual/integral/unity/oneness/wholeness/individual/unique/ universal.

Awake/conscious/aware/rational/intelligent/sentient/ perceptive/sensate.

Feeling/emotion/sensitivity/temperment/demeanor/manner/ propensity.

Inner truth/integrity/character/excellence/goodness/kindness/ humanness.

Viable/vital/mutable/transformative/developmental/ evolutional/migratory.

Gift/calling/*dharma*/vocation/originality/creativity/capacity/ potency/efficacy.

Virtuosity/ability/talent/aptitude/skill/knack/aptness/ ingenuity/genius/spirit.

Luminous/radiant/vibrant/charismatic/numinous/magnetic/ attractive.

Innermost/deepest/centermost/highest/utmost/greatest/fullest/ truest Self.

Inborn/inner Tao-nature/Spirit-nature/Heavenly-Earthly nature/naturalness.

A co-existing body-Spirit/Spirit-body/immanent and transcendent Tao/Spirit.

Considering the Human Soul evokes the dignity, mystery, miracle, marvel, magnificence, splendor and beauty of the sheer and utter and pure and simple reality, actuality and experience of Human Being and being human as embodied Spirit and inSpirited body.

Our Human Soul, as embodied Spirit and inSpirited body, is the ultimate and final alchemical refinement and transformation of the specious lead of our human ego from its over-identifying with the darkness, denseness, coarseness and separateness of the body, mind, others and world to the precious gold of our Human Self and its full-identifying *as* the lightness, subtleness, fineness and oneness of Spirit, Psyche, Beings and Multiverse.

The life-long journeying of our Human Soul and its many passages are a Soul-making/enSouling developmental alchemical transformative process that is itself the uncut, smoothly polished, crystalline philosopher's stone that transmutes our Human Being, Self and Living from the massive, broken, dull and pallid boulders of its ego's ignobility to the small, whole, brilliant and sparkling diamonds of its Spirit's nobility.

The Chinese characters for Soul are those for the twin Human Spiritual Soul/Hun and the physical Soul/P'o. Primordial Ch'i energy differentiates; ascending above as Great Yang and forming Heaven, Yang Ch'i energy and the Spiritual Soul/Hun of human beings and descending below as Great Yin and forming Earth, Yin Ch'i energy and the physical Soul/P'o of human beings.

At the beginning of human life, the Spiritual Soul descends from Heaven and the physical Soul ascends from Earth and, together, they constitute our Heavenly-Earthly Spiritual nature and being throughout our life course, life cycle and life span. At the ending of human life, the Spiritual Soul ascends, returning to Heaven, and the physical Soul descends, returning to Earth.

The co-existing, uniting and integrating of the Spiritual and physical twin Souls, as constituting our real and true inborn Spirit-nature/Virtuosity/Te as human beings, are the joining of Heaven/Spirit and Earth/our bodies *as* our body-Spirit, Spirit-body and Human Soul.

The following briefly summarizes the nature, qualities, characteristics, functions, relationships, activities and movements of the physical and Spiritual twin Souls:

PHYSICAL SOUL/P'O	SPIRITUAL SOUL/HUN
Body Soul	Breath Soul
Earthly/animal	Heavenly/Divine
Lower/inferior	Higher/superior
Form/sentience	Principle/faculties
Negative/passive	Positive/active
Regulates Soma	Regulates Psyche
Yin Ch'i energy	Yang Ch'i energy
Ascends from Earth at birth	Descends from Heaven at birth
Descends to Earth at death	Ascends to Heaven at death
Our embodied human Spirit	Our inSpirited human body
Our body-Spirit	Our Spirit-body
Incarnation/incorporation	Animation/activation

The Chinese character for Spirit/Ling is also defined as Soul. And the combined characters Hsin/Heart-Mind and Ling/Spirit are defined as Soul/Spirit/Mind, signifying that our Human Soul is our Spiritual Heart-Of-Hearts. These characters, like most English language definitions of Soul and Spirit, do not distinguish between them and include Mind and Psyche in the definitions.

Human beings who have a whole and full integration of the Spiritual and physical Human Souls are interested, attentive and receptive; accepting, appreciating and allowing; nourishing, supporting and encouraging and fostering, assisting and benefiting. Human beings who are closed off and shut down are disappointed, discouraged and disheartened and, for the most part, have only an inchoate and fragile animal-like, machine-like, robot-like and/or android-like 'soul' and are relatively soulless.

Human beings with vacuous souls generally live a rigid, routinized and mechanical and unfulfilling, incomplete and despairing life. Human beings with deep Soulfulness live an earthy, passionate and intimate and rich, meaningful and fulfilling life. They are embodying the inner openness, mildness, tenderness, goodness, fairness, kindness and gentleness of the Virtuosity/Te of Tao/Spirit that are personified and actualized in their gratitude, compassion, empathy, forgiveness and courage; that by which their pleasure, happiness, gladness, joy and delight are freely, openly, warmly, fully and wholeheartedly expressed and shared.

Again, in common parlance, human beings who have 'Soul' or are 'old Souls', 'good Souls' or 'kind Souls', are variously experienced as timeless and wise, real and intimate, true and genuine, warm and congenial, gifted and special, magnetic and attractive and cheerful and friendly and, as such, are usually respected, valued, loved, honored and cherished. They embody qualities of uniqueness, character, excellence, integrity, charisma, efficacious power, talented genius and radiant luminosity associated with the Virtuosity/Te of Tao/Spirit, their inner Tao/Spirit-nature, and with being 'enSouled' Human Beings.

Human beings who are Soulful, passionately put their whole Hearts and Souls into their being, living, relating, working and playing. Their intense commitment and devotion, often to a way of being or to an art form, contagiously arouse deep emotional feelings in us and they are inspiring, uplifting and elevating models of real, true and authentic human being.

Soul mates are lovers who have gratefully found their destined corresponding intimate partners from past lifetimes or in the present one. And, of course, there is the long history of Soul food and Soul music made by Soul sisters and Soul brothers in the African ancestral ethnic community that resonate deeply and warmly in the kindred Souls of all who partake and enjoy their gifts and offerings.

Lost Souls are human beings who have not yet discovered or consciously realized their gifts, calling, way or direction in life or their unique place, role and participation in the 'Anima Mundi' or World Soul and who have not yet awakened to the Sacred Spiritual and Soulful relationships within themselves between their body, mind, Heart, Soul and Spirit and between those of other human beings and living beings in the world, environment, cosmos and multiverse. In contrast, the Oversoul is the absolute reality and ground of existence identified as Spiritual Being whereby and wherein the ideal and essential Spiritual nature present in human beings is perfectly realized and fully manifested.

Often, Soul-retrieval assistance by indigenous and/or 'urban' shamans is required to liberate human beings from their attachments to, investments in, entanglements by and identifications with alluring and seductive sensory experiences of the external material/ physical world of 'others' and 'things'; and to awaken them from being immersed, absorbed, enmeshed and submerged in their sleep, dreams and nightmares; trances, illusions and delusions and fascinations, obsessions and frustrations with only the fleeting shadows and echoes of the Pure Light of Spiritual Reality and the Clear Sound of Soulful Truth.

And, fortunately, our Human Souls can resurrect/rise from the dead, undergo metempsychosis, transmigrate/pass from one body to another and reincarnate/be reborn in a new human body or life form. So, perhaps there are more opportunities for our Human Soul to transform and/or complete *karmic* issues; to be evolved enough to choose and intend its purpose, journey and destiny and to live a wiser, truer, freer and more Spiritual, Sacred and Soulful Human Life.

Integration of Soul

Our Human Soul is the co-existing integration of our human body and our Human Spirit. The following describes some of the attributes, characteristics, qualities and activities of our body-Spirit and our Spirit-body:

Body-Spirit/Physical Soul/P'o	Spirit-Body/Spiritual Soul/Hun
Incarnation/incorporation	Animation/activation
Soul is an embodied Spirit	Soul is an inSpirited body
Spirit endowed/suffused body	Body evolved/diffused Spirit
Soul is more body-identified	Soul is more Spirit-identified
More 'body' to Spirit and Soul	More 'Spirit' to body and Soul
Spirit progressively materializes in living over time	Body progressively dematerializes in living over time
Spirit becomes more body-like	Body becomes more Spirit-like
Spirit is more Earth/body-bound	Body is more Heaven/Spirit-bound
Body-bound Spirit is a source of Soul's constant sufficiency	Body-free Spirit is a re-source of Soul's potent proficiency
Spirit continues to descend and condense/coalesce to a lower/denser vibrational level/frequency	Body continues to ascend and radiate/evanesce to a higher/finer vibrational level/frequency
Spirit enters body at birth	Spirit exits body at death
Nascence/adolescence	Coalescence/senescence
Mystery/Miracles of originating/forming	Marvels/Magnificence of manifesting/completing
Birthing/growing	Maturing/transcending
More ego-identified with body/mind/others/world	More Self-identified with Spirit/Psyche/Beings/Universe

Tao/Spirit, Te/Human Soul, Ch'i/Human Energy

The following identifies some of the attributes, characteristics, qualities and activities of Tao as Spirit, Te as Human Soul and Ch'i as the Human Energy of Spirit and Soul:

Tao/Spirit/Shen	Ch'i/Energy	Te/Soul/Hun P'o
Ultimate Reality	Vital Energy	Intimate Actuality
Absolute Tao	Energetic Tao	Individualized Tao
Virtuality[6]	Viability	Virtuosity[6]
Potentiality	Vitality	Actuality
Creating/originating	Vitalizing/energizing	Incarnating/embodying
Animating/activating	Enlivening/vivifying	Individualizing/personifying
Potentiating/catalyzing	Nourishing/sustaining	Incorporating/inSpiriting
Principle/Essence	Primordial/endowed	Heavenly/Divine
Absolute/pure/free	Acquired/cultivated	Earthly/animal
Transcendent	Nonmaterial/rarefied	Spiritual/L. *animus*/Hun
Phenomenal/immanent[7]	Material/condensed	Physical/L. *anima*/P'o
Formless/evanescent	Transforming	Formed/coalescent
Undifferentiated	Moving/flowing	Differentiated
Relative/mixed/bound	Preserved/nourished	Yang/creative/fiery
Process/existence	Conserved/economized	Yin/receptive/watery
Multiplicity	All-constituting	Uniqueness
Diversity	All-pervading	Integrity
Unity	All-circulating	Potency
Identity	All-sustaining	Efficacy
Totality	All-completing	Excellence

Since English and Chinese dictionary definitions of 'Spirit' and 'Soul' often include 'psyche' and 'mind' and the Chinese language character 'Hsin' is defined as 'Heart-Mind'; in considering Spirit, our Human Soul and Energy; it may be of some heuristic value to include the following English language adjectives for states and qualities of 'heartedness' and 'mindedness'.

Faint-/hard-/cold-/heavy-/half-/broken-/down-/false-/
    cruel-hearted.
Single-/big-/large-/great-/stout-/brave-/lion-/ whole-/
    free-hearted.
Good-/pure-/true-/open-/light-/soft-/tender-/warm-/
kind-hearted.

Absent-/fuzzy-/feeble-/small-/weak-/simple-minded.
Low-/narrow-/tough-/closed-/wrong-/evil-minded.
Single-/sound-/clear-/open-/high-/right-minded.
Light-/tender-/fair-/broad-/social-/like-minded.

CHING

經

**LITERARY CLASSIC/SCRIPTURE/CANON
PASS THROUGH/UNDERGO/EXPERIENCE
STANDARD/REGULATE/TRANSACT
LONGITUDE/WARP/MERIDIANS/VEINS
CONSTANT/RECURRING**

**DEEP UNDERGROUND FLOWING WATER-
COURSES AND LONG INTERWEAVING
PASSAGEWAYS OF EXPERIENCING**

Ching as Human Passage

Conscious human living is replete with passages and passaging to, from and between various states, conditions, qualities and phenomena of being, existing, consciousness, awareness and experiencing. Living is a constant, continuous and continual flowing process that is natural, organic, sequential and seamless.

Dictionary definitions of 'passage(s)' describe them as actions or processes of transitioning or passing from one place or condition to another; travels, journeys and crossings and as openings and ways of entry, access and exit. Passageways are further defined as roads, paths, ways, channels and courses by or through which something passes.

Passages can be considered as 1) linear and one-way, where origins only lead to destinations, 2) linear and two-way where origins and destinations alternate back and forth between each other and 3) cyclical round trips where destinations return to origins after intermediate destinations and become new origins.

Passages in human consciousness are often understood, sought after, made and experienced as one-way, usually from an undeveloped, negative or undesirable state to a more developed, positive and desirable one, e.g., we ordinarily do not desire to passage from happiness to sadness. However, like the dynamic interchanging of Yin Ch'i/Yang Ch'i bipolar complements, passages are value neutral phases of a two-way, back and forth, alternating and reciprocal process of originating, reversing and returning, e.g., only being happy or sad is not true to the reality of experience. Passages are not so much a 'from one to another' but, rather, are a 'between the two' phenomena, e.g., we usually experience moving between happiness and sadness. And, as depicted by the Supreme Ultimate/T'ai Chi symbol, the seed potential of one phenomenon is latent within its bipolar complement, e.g., hidden within the actuality of happiness is the potentiality of sadness and vice versa, particularly when they reach their maximum.

The Chinese character 'Ching' is variously defined as classic book/literary classic/scripture/canon/standard/invariable rule/constant/recurring/regulate/transact/plan/arrange/pass by/pass through/experience/undergo/things running lengthwise/arteries/veins/meridians and its etymological radical and phonetic characters 'Ssu', 'Mi' and 'Ching' are defined as the longitudinal weaving of delicate floss silk loomthreads and the underground currents of deep flowing watercourses.

In this rendition of the *Tao Te Ching*, Ching is translated as 'Passage' and denotes the passages that our Human Soul undergoes and experiences in its Soul-work, Soul-making and Soul-journeying throughout our life course, life cycle and life span. So, in this Spirit/Soul-grounded, focused and centered rendition, Tao is Spirit, Te is our Human Soul and Ching are the passaging and passages of our Human Soul. The whole title of this rendition of the *Tao Te Ching* then reads as *Spirit Soul Passages* with the following meanings:

Tao/Spirit	Te/Soul	Ching/Passage
Ultimate Reality	Intimate Actuality	Our Human Soul's Passages
Heavenly/Divine	Earthly/Human	as the longitudinal floss silk
Universality	Individuality	threadings and underground
Transcendent Virtuality	Immanent Virtuosity	deep watercourse flowings
Primordial Ch'i	Acquired Ch'i	it continuously undergoes
Yang Ch'i Pole	Yin Ch'i Pole	and experiences as it passes
All That Is	As It Is	through the life of its human
Everywhere At Once	Right Here/Right Now	embodiment and transitions

Bipolar Experiental Passages

Several passages between the inner realities and outer manifestations of our Human Soul are found in the actual linguistic structure of some of the bipolar experiential concepts in the *Tao Te Ching* text. These are:

0. *Non-to Supreme Ultimate* — the passaging from the Ultimateless/Wu Chi to the Supreme Ultimate/T'ai Chi in the cosmogonic sequencing of Tao/Spirit.

1. *Tao to Virtuosity/Te* — the passaging from the Ultimate Reality of Tao/Spirit to its embodiment and personification as its Virtuosity/Te; the inner Tao/Spirit-nature, unique individuality, efficacious power, innate genius and radiant beauty of our Human Soul.

2. *Shaded/Yin Ch'i to Sunny/Yang Ch'i* — the passaging from the inner, deeper and receptive Yin Ch'i energies to the outer, higher and expressive Yang Ch'i energies of our Human Soul.

3. *Heaven/T'ien to Earth/Ti* — the passaging from the inner, vast and celestial dimension to the outer, localized and terrestrial dimension of our Human Soul.

4. *Nothing/Wu to Doing/Wei* — the passaging from our inner Non-Being and formless reality to the outer, being and form of the Tao/Spirit-sourced activities of our Human Soul.

5. *Spirit/Shen to Body/Shen* — the passaging from Spirit to our human body that is our Human Soul as an embodied Spirit or body-Spirit.

6. *Sacred/Sheng to Human Being/Jen* — the passaging from the Sacredness and wisdom of our inner Spiritual Being to the various personifications and identifications of our outer human being at the Center and Heart of our Human Soul.

7. *Body/Shen to Spirit/Ling* — the passaging from our human body to Spirit that is our Human Soul as an inSpirited body or Spirit-body.

8. *Experiencing/Ching to Journeying/Hsing* — the passaging from the undergoing of the ordinary and everyday living of our Human Soul to its conscious wayfaring journeying along a Path of Tao/Spirit.

9. *Wandering/Yu to Accompanying/P'ei* — the passaging from the solo meanderings of our Human Soul to the unity and identity of its more consciously intended, clearly focused, consistently guided and intimately shared Spiritual wayfaring.

10. *Self/Tzu to So/Jan* — the passaging from the naturalness and freedom of the inner Self of our Human Soul to its spontaneous presencing of-itself-so and *as*-itself-so in conscious awareness and experience.

11. *Everything/Wan to Beings/Wu* — the passaging from the myriad phenomena of the inner, subjective and potential consciousness of our Human Soul to the outer, objective and actual manifesting of the diverse beings, objects and things of its experiencing.

12. *All/I This/Tz'u to As/Ju This/Che* — the passaging from the reality, totality, ubiquity and simultaneity of Tao/Spirit to its actuality, locality and contemporaneity in/*as* our Human Soul.

13. *Ego/Wo to Self/Chi* — the passaging of our Human Soul from its exclusive ego-identification with body, mind, others and world to its inclusive Self-identifying as Spirit, Psyche, Beings and Multiverse.

14. *Death/Ssu to Immortality/Hsien* — the passaging of our Human Soul from the consummate finality and discontinuity of its transient mortal life to the ultimate destiny and continuity of its Eternal Immortal Life.

These bipolar experiential passages are described in greater detail as Essential Transformative Passages in Appendix Four of this rendition and include relevant opening excerpts, symbolic images, living processes, focused meditations and contemplative inquiries.

Transitional Pivots, Images and Living Processes

Like dawn and dusk and Spring and Autumn are, respectively, intermediate phases of diurnal alternations and seasonal cycles, so too do passages of the experiential concepts have transitional stages, mediating links and bridges and pivotal conveyances in their transformings. The following identifies some of these:

Experiential Concept	Transitional Pivot	Experiential Concept
Wu Chi/Non-Ultimate	Manifesting	T'ai Chi/Supreme Ultimate
Tao/Ultimate Reality	Individualizing	Te/Intimate Virtuosity
Yin Ch'i/Shady	Alternating	Yang Ch'i/Sunny
T'ien/Heaven	Human Being	Ti/Earth
Wu/Nothing	Flowing	Wei/Doing
Shen/Spirit	Body-Spirit	Shen/Body
Sheng/Sacred	Evolving	Jen/Human Being
Shen/Body	Spirit-Body	Ling/Spirit
Ching/Experiencing	Wayfaring	Hsing/Journeying
Yu/Wandering	Joining	P'ei/Accompanying
Tzu/Self	Spontaneity	Jan/So
Wan/Everything	Actuality	Wu/Beings
I/All Tz'u/This	Presence	Ju/As Che/This
Wo/Ego	Soul	Chi/Self
Ssu/Death	Life	Hsien/Immortality

Also, the passages of the experiential concepts have associated symbolic images and living processes as follows:

Passage	Symbolic Image	Living Process
Non- to Supreme Ultimate	Mystery/Hsuan	Originating/Yuan
Tao to Virtuosity	Mother/Mu	Birthing/Sheng
Yin Ch'i to Yang Ch'i	Breath/Ch'i	Vitalizing/Huo
Heaven to Earth	Soil/T'u	Grounding/Chi
Nothing to Doing	Water/Shui	Nourishing/Yang
Spirit to Body	Belly/Tu/Fu	Embodying/T'i
Sacred to Human Being	Heart/Hsin	Centering/Chung
Body to Spirit	Head/T'ou	InSpiriting/Ku
Experiencing to Journeying	Path/Lu	Wayfaring/Chin
Wandering to Accompanying	Union/Ho	Identifying/T'ung
Self to So	Child/Tzu	Playing/Wan
Everything to Beings	Home/Chia	Returning/Fan
All This to As This	Wheel/Lun	Culminating/Chung/Ch'uan/Ch'eng
Ego to Self	Light/Kuang	Awakening/Wu
Death to Immortality	Transition/Kuo	Destining/Ming

As noted above, these passages are described in greater detail in Appendix Four of this rendition.

Each one of the 81 Passages of the *Tao Te Ching/Spirit Soul Passages* text is a rendering that identifies its Spirit and Soul meaning and is titled to reflect a particular passage identified in and selected from the text. The Soul-journeying commentaries for each of the rendered passages are introduced by a brief description from the text and are framed as questions to us, as journeying Human Souls, regarding possibilities of progressing from a less developed and less desirable ego-identified state to a more developed and more desirable Self-identified state that is Spirit-centered and Soul-focused.

The selected passages and related commentaries are not necessarily essential or exclusive ones and are by no means definitive or exhaustive. You are invited and encouraged to discover and identify other passages and questions that are, perhaps, more evident, interesting, relevant and/or meaningful for you.

The Middle Kingdom

The following are passages using eight main experiential concepts cited in this rendition of the *Tao Te Ching/Spirit Soul Passages* as the mediating 'Middle Kingdom', Heart Center and Pivotal Axis of Tao/Spirit between the respective bipolar realities, qualities, activities and relationships of ego-identified people and Self-identified Human Beings.

Ego-Identified Persons	Main Concept	Self-Identified Human Beings
Nonexistence	*Tao/Spirit*	Ultimate Reality
Nothing		No-'thing'-ness
Absence		Presence
Ego	*Te/Soul*	Inborn Tao/Spirit-nature
Personality		Unique individuality
Power		Virtuosity
Diverted	*Ch'i/Energy*	Cultivated
Wasted		Compounded
Blocked		Circulating
Separation	*Yin/Yang Ch'i*	Interdependence
Opposition		Complementarity
Conflict		Harmony
People	*Sheng Jen*	Sacred Human Beings
The Populace		Spiritual Human Beings
Others		Soulful Human Beings
Contriving	*Wu Wei Ch'i*	Yielding
Controlling		Flowing
Forcing		Following

Artificial	*Tzu Jan*	Natural
Rehearsed		Spontaneous
Repeated		Novel

Things	*Wan Wu*	Beings
Objects		Selves
Entities		Souls

Meditative concentration on, reflection on, contemplation of and absorption in the 'Middle Kingdom', Heart Center and Pivotal Axis of Tao/Spirit of these main experiential concepts can assist and facilitate becoming awakened to and aware of their bipolarity, integrating them, transitioning between them and transforming them from their Spiritually/Soulfully less evolved to their Spiritually/Soulfully more evolved states, qualities, characteristics, attributes, activities and relationships.

Soul Journeying – 1

Most all transformative developmental processes go through four interrelated stages of:

1. *The Mystery of originating* — creating matter/something from No-'thing'.

2. *The Miracle of forming* — inner materializing of physical boundaries/limits/edges.

3. *The Marvel of manifesting* — outer appearing of uniquely individualized being/form.

4. *The Magnifence of completing* — culminating of growing/developing/maturing.

Prime examples are:
1. Seed ovule/germinating, sprouting/blossoming/foliation and/or fruition.
2. Larval caterpillar/cocoon, pupa, chrysalis/emerging/imago or winged butterfly.
3. Fertile egg/incubating/hatching/fully grown chicken.
4. Conception/fetation, gestation, pregnancy/parturition, birthing/mature being.

And other transformative processes such as:
1. Pathogen infection/incubation/symptom appearance/ disease treatment and cure.
2. Seed sewing/tending, cultivating/growing, developing, ripening/harvesting.
3. Unrefined base material, 'lead'/alchemical transmutation, e.g., calcination, liquefaction, distillation, coagulation, etc./ refined noble material, 'gold'.
4. Initiating therapy/inner transforming/outer manifesting/ terminating therapy.

The Spiritual journeying of our Human Soul correlates with progressive developmental stages that we, as human beings, go through during and throughout our human life course, life cycle and life span, e.g.,

Mystery	Miracles	Marvels	Magnificence
Of creation/ origination	Of formation/ transformation	Of emergence/ manifestation	Of completion/ culmination
of life/being	of body/fetus	of person/self	of Spirit/Soul
Impregnation/ conception	Gestation/ fetation	Parturition/ birthing	Development/ maturation

Childhood	Youth	Young Adulthood	Old Adulthood
Initiating	Developing	Uniting	Consummating
Nascence/	Pubescence/	Coalescence/	Senescence/
renascence/	adolescence/	concrescence/	canescence/
recrudescence	juvenescence	hyalescence	increscence
Being new/	Growing up/	Integrating/	Being old/
coming into life	forming life	enacting life	going out of life
Luminescing/	Florescing/	Incandescing/	Phosphorescing/
fluorescing	efflorescing	candescing	evanescing
Radiating light/	Flowering/	Radiating heat/	Enduring light/
shining aura	blossoming	glowing warmth	vanishing vapor

Words that are using the noun and adjective suffixes of '-escence' and '-escent' (Latin *-escens/-escent/-escentia*) denote the initial, inchoative, formative and slight process, qualities and states of the beginning, beginning to be, becoming and being of something, especially the reflecting, emitting and radiating of light.

Such words; and related ones such as antecedence, descendence, precedence, ascendence and transcendence; quintessence, essence, presence, lucence and translucence and innocence, magnificence, munificence and beneficence; are aptly suited to describe some states of Soulful being that may be occurring or present at certain stages in, or for certain of us human beings during, the human life course, life cycle and life span of our Soul-journeying, e.g.,

Iridescence/opalescence/pearlescence — the state of being that is the embodied, focused play and orderly array of the colorful spectral, prismatic and rainbow-like emitted luminous energy and the lustrous radiant light of Spirit visibly occurring at the cellular level; and that is one of shining forth in the etheric bodies and auras of living beings from their very beginning.

Effervescence/incalescence/recalescence — the state of being that is full of life; awake, crisp, brilliant and radiant; warm and glowing; gladdened, cheerful, joyful and enthusiastic;

animated, lively, energetic and spirited; ardent, fervent and passionate and stimulating, refreshing, invigorating and exhilerating; and that is one of freshness, vitality, vibrancy and vivacity.

Virescence/viridescence — the state of being that is greenish in life; child-like in the sense of being naive, innocent and trusting; curious, interested and playful; natural, open and spontaneous; unripe in development, experience and judgment; and that is one of curiosity, discovery and learning and the assimilating, integrating and enjoying of novelty.

Acquiescence/defervescence — the state of being that is one with life; cooling down; accepting, attuning and according; adjusting, adapting and conforming; accomodating, surrendering and complying; yielding, allowing and following; and that is one of giving in and over to that which is natural, essential, necessary, appropriate, fitting and suitable.

Decrescence/detumescence — the state of being that is decreasing in life; becoming less by gradually giving up needs, relinquishing habits, simplifying complexities, lessening reactivity, diminishing attachments, reducing possessions, eliminating ownership; and that is one of feeling adequate and sufficient by having very little clutter, filler and baggage.

Quiescence/arborescence — the state of being that is quiet in life; rooted and growing tree-like; serene, tranquil, peaceful and at rest; still, stable, steady and calm; contented, relaxed, at ease and comfortable; secure, carefree, leisurely and unhurried; and that is one of equanimity and freedom from anxiety, stress, disturbance, strife, agitation and turmoil.

Convalescence/reflorescence — the state of being that is recovering life; gradually recuperating and rehabilitating after illness, injury, wounding and weakness; regenerating energy and regaining vitality; restoring health, reconstituting self and renewing life; and that is one of returning to well-being, strength, efficacy, blossoming, flowering and flourishing.

Concupiscence — the state of being that is desiring in life; wanting, wishing, longing, yearning and hoping; needing, hungering, thirsting and craving; coveting and lusting; greediness, avarice and cupidity; striving, efforting and struggling; and that is one that can be strong, intense, urgent, persistent, tenacious, extreme, excessive, inordinate and unrelenting.

Tumescence/intumescence/turgescence — the state of being that is the swelling of life; dilated, distended and bulging; egocentric, egotistical and self-important; puffed up, inflated and grandiose; prideful, conceited and arrogant; and that is one of a thinning and weakening enlargement of the ego from internal pressure and expanding beyond its normal limits.

Spinescence/frutescence/rufescence — the state of being that is spiny in life; thorny, prickly and shrubby; abounding with difficulties, obstacles and annoyances; enduring ticklish, touchy and sensitive situations, issues and relationships; and that is one of flushing with shame, blushing with embarassment and reddening with irritation, inflammation and anger.

Obsolescence/excrescence/putrescence — the state of being that is unused in life; unessential, extraneous and irrelevant; insignificant, unimportant and inconsequential; outdated, outmoded and vestigial; disregarded, rejected and discarded; and that is one of being meaningless, useless, worthless, stale, moldy, rancid, musty and foul.

Deliquescence/liquescence — the state of being that is flowing with life; progressively softening, liquifying and washing away solid ego-formations, defenses and resistances; fixed conceptions and truths; rigid ego-investments and attachments; sclerotic habits, patterns and routines; and that is one of cleansing, purifying, clearing, opening, nourishing and sustaining.

Reminiscence — the state of being that remembers life; recalling, recollecting and reminding; reviving, restoring and renewing; returning, re-imagining and reflecting; appreciating, integrating and cherishing in mind, conscious awareness, memory and heart; and that is one of giving Soulful attention to and not forgetting memorable previous experience.

Rejuvenescence/reviviscence — the state of being that is renewing life; reviving, revitalizing and reinvigorating; reawakening, reigniting and rekindling; recharging, reanimating and reactivating; re-creating, replenishing and refreshing Spirit, deep Heart and Soul and Higher Self and that is one of renovating aliveness, freshness, softness and youthfulness.

The developmental stages and some of the states of being identified above, and many others not here identified, in the journeying of our Human Soul throughout its life course, life cycle and life span are consciously and continually experienced by fully awake and clearly aware human beings who are naturally and freely being and living the splendorous advent, presencing and epiphany of their embodied Spirit, inSpirited body and Human Soul and its Mysterious originating, Miraculous forming and transforming, Marvelous manifesting and Magnificent completing.

Soul Journeying – 2

Soul journeying is progressing from predominantly identify-ing with being a body/mind in a world of things/egos/others to predominantly identifying *as* being a Spirit/Consciousness in a Universe of Beings/Selves/Human Beings. The en-Souling jour-ney of human living is an ad-venture/advent-ure that endows, imbues and infuses our Human Being with a Soul throughout our life course, life cycle and life span. It is moving from a solid ground and minute dimensionless still point to a clear space and vast circumferenceless open circle mediated by and occurring in the empty center and integral pivotal axis of our Human Heart.

The following is a symbolic visual representation of our inte-gral Human Soul:

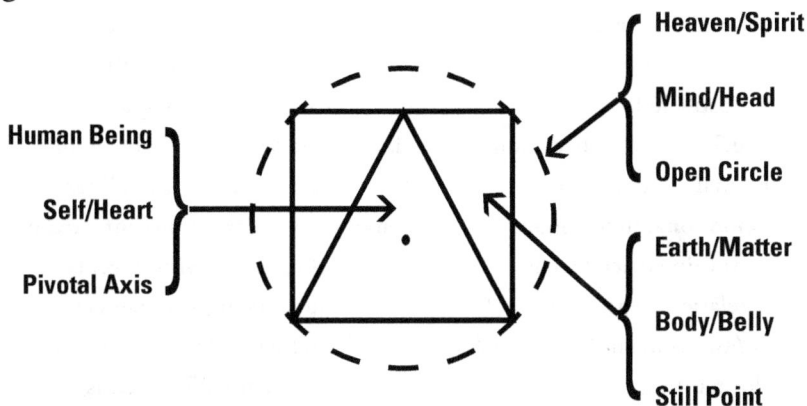

which can be meditated upon to experience its co-existing actuality.

The en-Souling journey involves a wide variety of moving, passaging and transitioning; changing, transforming and trans-muting; growing, developing and evolving and shifting, trans-posing and migrating that support, assist and facilitate our Human Soul in its coalescing, deepening, unfolding, expanding, radiating and shining forth.

Soul Journeying – 3

The following are some of the transformative passages of the enSouling journeying process.

From	To
Earthly-nature	Heavenly-nature
Physical-nature	Spiritual-nature
Body/mind/ego	Spirit/Psyche/Self
Others/people	Beings/Human Beings
World/environment	Cosmos/universe
Body-bound existing	Spirit-freed living
Solid ground/still point	Clear space/open circle
No dimension/minute	No circumference/vast
ego-thing/entity	Spirit-Being/identity
Abstracted/separated/	Concretized/integrated/
externalized/objectified things/	internalized/personified phenomena/
mental contents/concepts	mental realities/actualities
emotional items/goods	emotional interrelations/interactions
volitional acts/deeds	volitional activities/events
relational egos/others	relational beings/human beings
Lost/asleep/dreaming/absent/	Found/awake/aware/present/
dormant/latent/bound in	active/manifest/free as
body/mind/ego/others/world	Spirit/Psyche/Self/Beings/Universe

EnSouling

Soul-journeying involves Soul-work that is Soul-making or 'EnSouling', the endowing and imbuing of our human being and living with/*as* a Human Soul. The life-long wayfaring of our human Self returning to Tao/Ultimate Reality is synonymous with, and identical to, the life-long journeying of our human ego returning to Spirit as a Human Soul through any number of its many passages.

Soul-journeying and the enSouling process go through passages, transformtions and progressions from and to:

Originating/creating/animating/activating
Vitalizing/energizing/potentiating/catalyzing
Nourishing/maintaining/sustaining/regulating
Developing/expanding/evolving/maturing
Concluding/completing/consummating/culminating

Soul-journeying, Soul-work, Soul-making and enSouling are the progressive awakening, cultivating, refining and unfolding of our rational, sentient, Spiritual and Divine inner-nature, often through 'dark nights of the Soul'; the deeply transforming and profound life-changing ego-deaths that open the way to mystical union with the Divine, identification *as* Spirit and Human Soul and living a real and true Human life joining and sharing with all human and living beings.[5]

Soul-journeying and the enSouling process go through developmental passages, transformings and progressions from ego-identifying with the body, mind, others and the world to Self- identifying with/*as* Spirit, Psyche, Being and the Multiverse; finally integrating our human body and Spirit and uniting an embodied Spirit and an inSpirited body; as a body-Spirit, Spirit-body and Human Soul.

EnSouling is the Soul-journeying of our Human Soul from being ego-identified, through being Self-identifying, to being

Spirit-identified *as* a Human Soul, a co-existing and integrated embodied Spirit and inSpirited body. The following identifies some attributes, characteristics, qualities and activities of ego-identified people and Spirit-identified human beings:

Ego-Identified People and Spirit-Identified Human Beings – 1

Ego-identified people tend to be more identified with body, mind, ego, others and world and Spirit-identified human beings tend to be more identified with Spirit, Psyche, Self, Beings and Universe. One way of considering Soul-journeying, Soul-work and Soul-making/EnSouling is the transforming passaging from some of the attributes, characteristics, qualities and activities of ego-identifying to some of those of Spirit-identifying, i.e., moving from being less ego-centered and ego-focused to being more Spirit-centered and Spirit-focused during the process of living, growing, developing and evolving.

Acknowledging the pitfalls of making what appear to be absolute and mutually exclusive generalizations about co-existing, interrelated, very fluid and ever changing human characteristics, the following are some for extreme ego-identified people and Spirit-identified human beings:

Ego-Identified People	Spirit-Identified Human Beings
Masses/Populace/Herd	Individual/Unique/Singular
Asleep/Unaware/Inattentive	Awake/Aware/Attentive
Unconscious/Unenlightened	Conscious/Enlightened
Ego-Centered/Other-Focused	Spirit-Centered/Soul-Focused
Outer-Directed/Object-Oriented	Inner-Directed/Intersubjective-Oriented
Conformist/Conventional	Non-Conformist/Unconventional
Unreal/Untrue/Inauthentic	Real/True/Authentic
Conditioned/Dependent	Unconditioned/Interdependent
Egotistic/Materialistic	Humanistic/Non-Materialistic
Mechanistic/Reductionistic	Vitalistic/Holistic
Ungrounded/Uncentered	Grounded/Centered
Separated/Divided	United/Undivided
Fragmented/Disconnected	Integrated/Connected
Dualistic/Either-Or/Exclusive	Non-Dual/Both-And/Inclusive
Partial/Incomplete	Whole/Complete
Attached/Invested	Non-Attached/Non-Invested
Occupied/Busy/Unavailable	Empty/Still/Available
Bound/Limited	Unbound/Unlimited
Closed/Distant	Open/Close
Narrow/Contracted	Broad/Expansive
Rigid/Inflexible	Fluid/Flexible
Insufficient/Discontented	Sufficient/Contented
Inadequate/Insecure	Adequate/Secure
Least Developed/Evolved	Most Developed/Evolved
Disembodied Spirit/Terror	Embodied Spirit/Body-Spirit
Despirited Body/Horror	InSpirited Body/Spirit-Body
Spiritless/Soulless	Spiritual/Soulful

Ego-Identified People and Spirit-Identified Human Beings – 2

Some further distinctions between ego-identified people and Spirit-identified human beings are the following ones:

Ego-Identified People	Spirit-Identified Human Beings
Encumbered/entrapped in a mortal body	Liberated as an immortal Spirit
Enamored/engrossed in a busy mind	Envisioning as a vast Psyche
Enveloped/encapsulated in a separate ego	Evolving into a nondual/integral Self
Engulfed/embroiled in alienated others	Interrelating with intimate Beings
Entangled/enmeshed in a limited world	Expanding into an infinite Multiverse
Embedded/entrenched in a transient life	Participating in an eternal Life
Enervated/enfeebled in wasted activities	Experiencing inexhaustible Energy
Enduring trials/sufferings/agonies	Enjoying blessings/gifts/delights

EnSouling human beings are generally avoiding and withdrawing from being distracted by, seduced by, fascinated with, entranced by, attached to and invested in the external sensory world of only the derivative and insubstantial shadows, echoes and images of the Pure Light, True Word and Ultimate Reality of Spirit and our Human Soul. They are fully, completely and Soulfully identifying with/*as* being an Energy-body, embodied Spirit, inSpirited body and Spirit-Being.

EnSouling human beings are acknowledging the past lives and incarnations and the future rebirths and reincarnations of our Human Soul beyond the apparent boundaries of its birthing, living and dying in the reality and actualities of present space-time. They are experiencing our Human Soul, not as Spirit confined and limited by its embodiment, but, rather, as the deeply-rooted ground, widely-ranging center and vastly-reaching space of its absolute freedom.

If any prefix denotes and epitomizes the viability, vitality, virtuality, Virtuosity and variability of our Human Soul and its many attributes, characteristics, qualities and activities; it is that of 'trans-' (Latin *trans-/tra-*) meaning 'across/through/beyond/ so as to change on or to the other side'. Words that use the prefix 'trans-' are particularly suited to identify some of the many vicissitudes and variations of the freedom of our Human Soul, e.g.,

Transgressions/transactions/transitions/transitoriness.

Transparency/translucence/transphenomenality/
transpersonality/transcendence.

Transformations/transmutations/transubtantiations/
transfigurations/transmogrifications.

Transmigrations/transplantations/translocations/
transpositions.

Transductions/transmissions/transferences/transfusions.

HSUAN   MIAO

玄   妙

DARK/DARKNESS/BLACK	WONDERFUL/MARVELOUS/EXCELLENT
DEEP/PROFOUND/ABYSMAL	GRACEFUL/BEAUTIFUL/ADMIRABLE
ABSTRUSE/OBSCURE/SUBTLE	FINE/EXQUISITE/MAGICAL
MYSTERY/MYSTERIOUS	MYSTERY/MYSTERIOUS
SECRET/HIDDEN	SECRET/SUBTLE

MYSTERY AND MARVELS ARE SYNONYMOUS WITH TAO/SPIRIT. MYSTERY IS 'DARK' TO ORDINARY EGO-CONSCIOUSNESS WHICH CANNOT ENCOMPASS OR GRASP ITS NON-BEING AND TOTALITY. MYSTERY IS TRANSCENDENT TAO/SPIRIT'S SECRET, CONCEALED IN THE TRANSPHENOMENAL DIMENSION; TOO DEEP, PROFOUND AND ABYSMAL; TOO VAST, BOUNDLESS AND LIMITLESS TO BE FATHOMED, COMPREHENDED AND EXPERIENCED. MARVEL, TOO, IS MYSTERIOUS, SECRET AND SUBTLE BUT IT ALSO IS IMMANENT TAO/SPIRIT'S BEAUTY, REVEALED IN THE PHENOMENAL WORLD; SO FINE, EXCELLENT AND EXQUISITE; SO WONDERFUL, MAGICAL AND GRACEFUL TO BE BEHELD, ADMIRED AND EXPERIENCED.

TRANSFORMATIVE PASSAGE 1

MYSTERY TO MARVELS

❖

Spirit being inSpirited is a counterpart of Infinite-Eternal Spirit
Its names being reputed are counterparts of its
Infinite-Eternal Name

Spirit's unnamable Non-Being is preceding Heaven-Earth
Spirit's named Being is Mother of all beings

Being thought-free is glimpsing Spirit's Eternal Mystery
Being thought-full is beholding Spirit's Infinite Miracles

Spirit's Mystery and Miracles are one and the same
And are only being named differently

This Identity is Spirit's Ultimate Mystery
Most dark, most deep, Mystery upon Mystery
Gateway of all Spirit's Wondrous Marvels

EXPLICATIVE SUMMARY ❖ 1

This passage is from our Human Soul's Mysterious originating to its Marvelous manifesting. Spirit is Infinite and Eternal and not objectifiable and namable. The Great Mystery of Spirit reveals itself in the originating, forming, manifesting and completing of the myriad, rich and varied Miracles, Marvels and Magnificence of our human being, existing and experiencing. Spirit's Mystery is Soul's Marvel concealed and Soul's Marvels are Spirit's Mystery revealed.

Spirit-identifying human beings experience both the Spirit-originating Mystery and the Spirit-forming Miracles of their lives as they manifest and complete the Marvels and Magnificence of their Soul-journeying.

MEDITATIVE INQUIRY ❖ 1[8]

As journeying Souls, can we:
Use our finite, temporal and diverse experiences to remember and return to Infinite, Eternal and Constant Spirit as the one Mysterious origin and destination of all life, how the namable beings and somethings come from, re-present and return to the unnamable Non-Being and No-thingness of Spirit?

Be thought-full and behold the Infinite Miracles of Spirit and be thought-free and glimpse the Eternal Mystery of Spirit and experience them as one Identity and the Ultimate Mystery of Spirit?

Remember that even the most disasterous, tragic, traumatic, abusive and damaging life experiences originate in, and manifest as, that same awesome, amazing, astonishing, wondrous and marvelous Great Mystery of Spirit?

Experience ourselves and fellow human beings as Miraculous and Marvelous incarnations and personifications of Mysterious Spirit; Soulfully regard and relate to each other *as* embodied Spirit and inSpirited bodies and respect, honor and cherish each other with inviolate dignity and integrity throughout our Human Soul-journeying?

TRANSFORMATIVE PASSAGE 2

DUALITY TO BIPOLARITY

❖

As ego-identifying people:
When we are conceiving of beauty
We are simultaneously invoking non-beauty
When we are conceiving good
We are simultaneously invoking non-good

Being and Non-Being are co-creating each other
Difficult and easy are contrasting each other
Long and short are comparing each other
High and low are complementing each other
Music and voice are composing each other
Before and after are completing each other

As Spirit-identifying human beings, we are:
Influencing activities without doing any 'thing'
Revealing learnings without teaching any 'thing'

As Spirit-identifying human beings, we are:
Attending whatever is happening
Supporting without possessing
Assisting without controlling
Accomplishing without crediting

As Spirit-identifying human beings
We are not requiring gratitude
Work is being completed and forgotten

EXPLICATIVE SUMMARY ❖ 2

This passage is from our Human Soul's many dualities to their bipolarity. The many dualities of our human existence and experience are bipolar interdependent complements rather than separate dualistic opposites that are one-sided and mutually exclusive. Spirit-identifying human beings are Soulfully attentive, supporting, assisting and accomplishing without soullessly possessing, controlling, crediting or 'doing' any 'thing' and are completing aspects of their Soul-work and forgetting about them without requiring gratitude.

MEDITATIVE INQUIRY ❖ 2

As journeying Souls, can we:

Pair up seemingly discrete individual experiences with their bipolar complements, e.g., experience happiness *and* sadness, love *and* hatred, life *and* death as two inseparable sides of the same coin of Spirit and find the positive blessings, gifts and opportunities in negative experiences without denying or rationalizing them?

If invoking fellow human beings as 'others'; attend to, Soulfully support and assist them as Human Souls rather than be soullessly possessive, controlling and manipulative and, if positive influencing and meaningful learning occur in Soul-work, acknowledge accomplishments and forget about them without taking credit or expecting gratitude?

Resolve conflicted relationships with fellow human beings whom we regard as 'others', adversaries, opponents and enemies to reject, beat, defeat or kill; by finding them within our own Human Soul, integrating our relationship, forgiving their actions and even being grateful for their presence in our lives and their contributing to our Soul-work and Soul-making?

Be and live the bipolar unity and nondual identity of apparent dualities and put an end to the childhood abuse, domestic violence, class struggles, racial prejudice, partisan politics, border disputes, religious wars and other human tragedies that are predicated upon various forms of dualistic, mutually exclusive and either-or human inequality and inequity that displace Spirit and plague our Human Souls?

TRANSFORMATIVE PASSAGE 3

ATTACHMENT TO NON-INTERFERING

❖

As ego-identified people, when we are:
Not exalting developed human beings
We are not competing
Not treasuring rare objects
We are not stealing
Not displaying desirable goods
Our heart-minds are not longing

As Spirit-identifying human beings
When we are regulating
Heart-minds are emptying
Belly centers are filling
Ambitious wills are weakening
Supporting bones are strengthening

As Spirit-identifying human beings
We are guiding ego-identified people
To be conceptless and desireless
And cleverness and craftiness
To be ineffective

By practicing non-interfering
This Spirit-State is self-regulating

EXPLICATIVE SUMMARY ❖ 3

This passage is from our Human Soul's mental and emotional attachments to its non-interfering actions and activities. Glorifying human beings, reifying concepts, satiating desires and worshiping things involve creating dualities, valuations, judgments, preferences, investments and attachments that result in imitation and competition, illusions and delusions, idolatry and envy and greed and thievery. Spirit-identifying human beings are assisting fellow human beings in the Soul-work of clearing mental concepts, emptying emotional desires and stilling volitional strivings and the strengthening of inner and deeper instinctual 'knowings' and 'doings' without interfering.

MEDITATIVE INQUIRY ❖ 3

As journeying Souls, can we:

Disidentify and detach from our ego's concepts of exalted others, desires for treasured objects and engagements in materialistic pursuits in the outer world of external 'things'?

Open the way to discovering, experiencing and esteeming the absolutely unique and incomparable individuality of our inborn Spirit-nature and Human Soul?

Allow the radiant beauty, abundant wealth and potentiating energy of Spirit and our Human Soul to shine forth, overflow and suffuse into our hearts, minds and bodies; affording us true security, sufficiency, satisfaction and serenity?

In Soul-work and Soul-making, be even free of concepts of Spirit and desires for Soul and guide fellow human beings to be and do so without using clever schemes and crafty strategies that interfere with the natural Spiritual self-regulating of their open-hearted inner Soul-journeying?

TRANSFORMATIVE PASSAGE 4

COMPENSATING TO HARMONY

❖

Spirit is a State of empty harmony
Using it is never exhausting it
It is this deep and vast
Unfathomable Source of all beings

It is:
Smoothing our sharp edges
Loosening our tight knots
Softening our bright lights
Settling our dusty worlds

Deep, still, pure, clear
It is remaining forever

Its origin is not known
It is existing before all beginnings
Before even Supreme Beings

EXPLICATIVE SUMMARY ❖ 4

This passage is from our Human Soul's compensating dynamics to its balancing harmony. The original State of Spirit is the pure, clear, deep and still Non-Being, No-thingness, vastness and emptiness of its Great and Eternal Mystery and is the Source, harmony, natural equality and perfect compensating and counterbalancing of the myriad bipolar relationships within our human existence, consciousness, experience, inborn Spirit-nature and Soul. Spirit-identified human beings are allowing the sharp edges, tight knots, bright lights and dusty worlds of their ego to naturally counterbalance, smoothen, loosen, soften and settle into a Soulful state of harmony and emptiness.

MEDITATIVE INQUIRY ❖ 4

As journeying Souls, can we:
Smooth the sharpness, loosen the tightness, soften the brightness and settle the dustiness of our egos and open the way to experiencing the profundity, purity, clarity and serenity of eternal Spirit and our inborn Spirit-nature and Human Soul?

Identify with/*as* the deep, vast and inexhaustible original empty harmony of Spirit and create an inner Soulful ground and center that allow all of the extremes of apparently separate and one-sided dualities of our experience to naturally counterbalance, compensate for each other and restore our Spirit's original state of equilibrium, centeredness and peacefulness?

TRANSFORMATIVE PASSAGE 5

IMPARTIALITY TO CENTRALITY

❖

The Spirit of Heaven-Earth is being impartial
By regarding all beings as sacrificial offerings
As Spirit-identifying human beings, we are being impartial
By regarding all ego-identified people as sacrificial offerings

The Spirit of Heaven-Earth's centerspace
Is being like a bellows
Empty and inexhaustible
The more it is pumping
The more it is generating

Many words are displacing emptiness
Most developed is identifying *as*
Spirit's Empty Center

EXPLICATIVE SUMMARY ❖ 5

This passage is from our Human Soul's impartiality to its empty centrality. Spirit is empty, open, centralized, nonpersonal, impartial and inexhaustibly generating. Spirit-identifying human beings are being impartial in relation to beings and fellow human beings and are silently and quietly centered in Spirit's emptiness and openness.

MEDITATIVE INQUIRY ❖ 5

As journeying Souls, can we:

Humbly, quietly and resolutely identify with/*as* Spirit, our inborn Spirit-nature and Human Soul, and Soulfully regard and relate to each other with equality, impartiality and equanimity?

Experience our human being as a great Holy-making sacrifice and humble offering to the greater whole Reality of Spirit and live our precious human lives openly, silently, quietly and creatively centered in the universe, Spirit, our Heart-of-Hearts and Human Soul?

TRANSFORMATIVE PASSAGE 6

MATERNITY TO ETERNITY

❖

Valley Spirit is never dying out
She is subtly and profoundly Feminine

The gateway of this Mysterious Feminine
Is the Root-Source of Heaven-Earth

She is everpresencing and everlasting
Utilizing Her is never wearing out

EXPLICATIVE SUMMARY ❖ 6

This passage is from our Human Soul's maternal Nature to its eternal Being. Spirit is infinite, eternal and inexhaustible. Valley Spirit is the Mysterious Feminine and Great Mother who is the everpresencing Root-Source of Heaven-Earth, our Human Soul and all creation. Spirit-identifying human beings are identifying with/*as* its Feminine/Maternal/Valley nature and creative life-birthing energies.

MEDITATIVE INQUIRY ❖ 6

As journeying Souls, can we:

Identify with/*as* the Feminine Spirit and Great Mother, regardless of our sexual gender, and experientially understand the Creatrix and the primordial, deep, inexhaustible and everlasting Spiritual Source of all life and our Human Soul?

Identify with/*as* original, subtle and profound Spirit; that which exists everywhere and forever, and ourselves be creative, infinite, eternal and immortal Human Souls, just as we are, right here and right now?

TRANSFORMATIVE PASSAGE 7

SELF-INTEREST TO UNIVERSALITY

❖

The Spirit of Heaven-Earth is everlasting
Timeless and eternal
By not generating itself
By not living for itself

As Spirit-identifying human beings, we are:
Being absent and constantly presencing
Being behind and constantly progressing

As Spirit-identifying human beings, we are:
Having no ego-interests
And embodying Universal Soul

EXPLICATIVE SUMMARY ❖ 7

This passage is from our Human Soul's ego-interests to its universal Selfhood. Spirit is nondual, timeless and eternal; beyond birthing, living and dying and is not living for itself. Spirit-identifying human beings are an 'absent presence' and 'progressing background' and are free of ego-interests in Soul-work, Soul-making, enSouling and Soul-journeying.

MEDITATIVE INQUIRY ❖ 7

As journeying Souls, can we:

Identify with/*as* Spirit and Soulfully become one with, and identical to, every fellow human being and living thing in our world, cosmos and universe?

In our Soulful human relationships and activities, be free of ego-needs for self-preserving, self-defending, self-interest, self-glorifying and self-precedence?

Quietly and humbly enjoy being and sharing the universal Spirit, Human Soul and Deeper/Higher Self that, as real and true human beings, we all innately, inherently, intrinsically and naturally are?

TRANSFORMATIVE PASSAGE 8

CONTENDING TO BENEFITING

❖

Most developed goodness is being like water
Water is benefiting all beings without contending

Water is dwelling in depths ignored by people
And, so, is approximating Tao/Spirit

As water-like goodness, we are loving:
Earthiness in dwelling
Deepness in heart-mind
Naturalness in relating
Truthfulness in speaking
Orderliness in governing
Effectiveness in serving
Timeliness in activities

As water-like Spirit-identifying human beings
We are not contending
And there is no harming

EXPLICATIVE SUMMARY ❖ 8

This passage is from our Human Soul's contending with beings to its benefiting all of them. The goodness of Spirit is water-like in its non-contending with, and its beneficial sustaining of, all beings and life. Spirit-identifying human beings are like the goodness of flowing water in their loving of being grounded, deep, natural, truthful, orderly, effective, timely and beneficial to all beings and not being contending with nor harming any of them.

MEDITATIVE INQUIRY ❖ 8

As journeying Souls, can we:

Be water-like flowing in our Soulful human being, living and interrelating and identify with/*as*, embody and personify the goodness and beneficence of Spirit and our Human Soul?

Be close to earth, flowing, nourishing and sustaining life and not resist, conflict, compete or contend with fellow human beings and Human Souls?

Be, live and enjoy the earthiness, deepness, naturalness, truthfulness, appropriateness, effectiveness and timeliness of Spirit and, by our Soulful presence alone, benefit everyone and everything without harming anyone or anything?

TRANSFORMATIVE PASSAGE 9

OVERDOING TO WITHDRAWING

❖

Filling to the point of overflowing
Is not as developed as stopping in time
And conserving an empty space of Spirit

Honing to the point of oversharpening
Is not as developed as stopping in time
And preserving a solid edge of Soul

When jade and gold are filling our houses
We are needing to safeguard them
Taking pride in wealth and fame
Is bringing Soul's downfall and collapse

Withdrawing when Soul-work is completed
Such is Heaven's Spirit

EXPLICATIVE SUMMARY ❖ 9

This passage is from our Human Soul's overdoing activities to its timely withdrawing. Ending activities in an appropriately complete and timely manner avoids losing both the emptiness and availability of Spiritual space and the solidness and utility of Soulful form and is the working of Spirit and our Human Soul. Spirit-identifying human beings are not overdoing activities, are appropriately withdrawing from them in a timely manner when they are completed and are not priding in fame and wealth.

MEDITATIVE INQUIRY ❖ 9

As journeying Souls, can we:

Not overextend ourselves, not overdo activities, stop in time and, thus, be efficient and effective and conserve and preserve our Human Soul's life energies without dissipating or depleting them?

Not soullesly hoard wealth and parade fame and not overfill the inner openness, emptiness and spaciousness of Spirit and not over-work the inner solidness, fullness and sharpness of our Human Soul?

Embody Spirit, step back and be withdrawing when our activities naturally complete themselves without overdoing them and risking unfortunate conclusions and unhappy endings in our Soul-work and Soul-making?

WU

無

NO-/NOT-/NON-/UN-
WITHOUT
NOTHING/NO-'THING'

T'AI

太

SUPREME/GREATEST/UTMOST
HIGHEST/VERY TOP/SUMMIT
VERY/MUCH/EXTREMELY

CHI

極

ULTIMATE/UTMOST/EXTREME
GREATEST EXTENT/LIMIT
RIDGEPOLE/PEAK/VERY TOP
APEX/ZENITH/SUMMIT
BORDER/BOUNDARY/EDGE/END
FIRST PRINCIPLE
THE POLES (YIN AND YANG)

WU CHI

NON-ULTIMATE/LIMITLESS
NOTHINGNESS
UNDIFFERENTIATED VOID
FORMS INTO:
PRIMORDIAL CH'I ENERGY
AND T'AI CHI

T'AI CHI

SUPREME ULTIMATE LIMIT
THE GREAT TRIAD
INTEGRATION OF:
WU CHI/YIN CH'I/YANG CH'I
HEAVEN/EARTH/HUMAN BEING
VITALITY/ENERGY/SPIRIT

TRANSFORMATIVE PASSAGE 10

EMBODYING TO ENSOULING

❖

As Spirit-identifying human beings, we are:
Unifying our Heavenly-Earthly Souls
And embodying undivided Oneness
Conserving our Soul's vital energies
And embodying infant suppleness
Purifying our Soul's inner vision
And embodying perfect clearness

As Spirit-identifying human beings, we are:
Loving people and regulating the Spirit-State
Without knowing or doing anything unnatural

As Spirit-identifying human beings, we are:
Embodying maternal nature
Opening and closing gateways of Heaven
Illuminating internal dimensions
Without taking interfering actions

Birthing and nourishing beings
Supporting without possessing
Assisting without controlling
Developing without forcing
Is profoundly Mysterious Soul

EXPLICATIVE SUMMARY ❖ 10

This passage is from our Human Soul's embodying oneness, clearness and suppleness to its enSouling unifying, purifying and conserving. As human beings, we have a twin Soul; a physical material body-Soul and a nonphysical nonmaterial Spirit-Soul which, when consciously integrated, constitute our unified and nondual embodied Spirit and inSpirited body. Spirit-identifying human beings are unifying their twin Souls, conserving their Soul's vital energy and purifying their inner vision; are Soulfully being maternal, loving, illuminating, clear, flexible, nourishing, supporting, assisting, regulating and developing and are not soullessly being possessive, controlling, forcing or otherwise interfering in relating with fellow human beings and Human Souls.

MEDITATIVE INQUIRY ❖ 10

As journeying Souls, can we:

Consciously and energetically integrate our twin Human Souls and experience ourselves as an integral body-Spirit and Spirit-body?

Conserve our Soul's life energies and purify our Soul's inner vision and, in addition to its unity, embody the vitality, flexibility, purity and clarity of Spirit, our inborn Spirit-nature and Human Soul?

Soulfully regulate ourselves and love fellow human beings by being naturally free of intellectual concepts and purposeful actions that interfere with the workings of Spirit and the unfolding journeying of our Human Soul?

Embody our maternal Spiritual nature, illuminate our inner Human Souls and nourish, support, assist and develop fellow human beings without being soullessly possessive, controlling, manipulative and forcing?

Embody and enact our Mysterious Spirit-nature and Magnificent Human Soul?

TRANSFORMATIVE PASSAGE 11

SOLIDNESS TO EMPTINESS

❖

Thirty spokes are radiating from one unifying hub
A wheel's usefulness is its empty centerspace

Clay is being shaped, forming a vessel
A vessel's usefulness is its empty innerspace

Doors and windows are being cut out, making a room
A room's usefulness is its empty openspace

Benefit is obtaining
From the being of our body's
Solid outer form
Utility is obtaining
From the Non-Being of Spirit's
Empty inner space

EXPLICATIVE SUMMARY ❖ 11

This passage of our Human Soul is from the solidness of its outer bodily forms to the emptiness of its inner Spritual space. Benefit is obtaining from the materiality and form of our body and utility is obtaining from the nonmateriality and formlessness of Spirit. Spirit-identifying human beings are beneficially and usefully integrating the being of their solid, closed and outer physical form and the non-being of their empty, open and inner Spiritual space and are being an embodied Spirit and an inSpirited body.

MEDITATIVE INQUIRY ❖ 11

As journeying Souls, can we:

Fully experience being a useful Spirit-like and beneficial Soulful human being by balancing and harmoniously integrating the empty and open inner centerspace of our Spiritual consciousness and the solid outer form of our physical body, being an embodied Spirit and an inSpirited body and a living Human Soul?

Be grounded in our body, centered in our Heart and clear in our mind and create a still, empty and open inner centerspace that is a beneficial foundation and useful expanse for experiencing the limits and possibilities of being a fully Spiritual human being and living a deeply Soulful human life?

TRANSFORMATIVE PASSAGE 12

SENSATION TO INWARDNESS

❖

As ego-identified people:
Many colors are blinding our eyes
Many sounds are deafening our ears
Many tastes are numbing our palates

Hunting and chasing are crazing our heart-minds
Getting and keeping are impeding our Soul's developing

As Spirit-identifying human beings, we are:
Attending to belly not eyes
Rejecting the outer *'that'*/ego
Accepting the inner *'This'*/Spirit

EXPLICATIVE SUMMARY ❖ 12

This passage is from our Human Soul's sensory experiencing to its Spritual inwardness. Overstimulating, saturating and overwhelming ourselves with intense external sensory input blinds, deafens and numbs Spirit and our Human Soul. Spirit-identifying human beings are not soullessly pursuing, acquiring and possessing the sensory-based objects of the external world of ego-experience and are, instead, cultivating the Spirit-based realities of the inner world of our Human Soul.

MEDITATIVE INQUIRY ❖ 12

As journeying Souls, can we:
Detach from soullessly seeking, pursuing, acquiring and perpetuating sensory-based, stimulation-driven, excitation-inducing and arousal-promoting experiences that are powerful distractions, deflections, diversions and deviations for Soul-work, Soul-making and Soul-journeying along the pathways of Spirit?

Experience stabilizing our bodies, calming our minds, regulating ourselves, nourishing our Human Soul and preserving Spirit by shifting away from being soullessly attracted by and directed toward superficial objects 'out there' in the external physical world to being focused upon and centered in deeper realities 'in here' in the internal Spiritual and Soulful universe?

Enjoy the resultant substantiality, sanity, security and serenity of our Body, Mind, Deeper and Higher Self, Human Soul and Spirit?

Transformative Passage 13

Favor to Trustworthiness

❖

Be fearing favor like fearing disgrace
Be regarding our selves as great trouble

What is meant by:
Fearing favor like fearing disgrace?
Favor is dishonoring and demeaning
We are afraid of losing it
We are afraid of having it
This is why favor, like disgrace,
Is frightening

What is meant by:
Regarding our selves as great trouble?
We are having great trouble
Because we are having an ego-self
If we are being Spirit's No-Self
We are having no trouble

Valuing all beings as our true Soul
We can be trusted by all beings
Loving all beings as our true Soul
We can be entrusted with all beings

EXPLICATIVE SUMMARY ❖ 13

This passage is from our Human Soul's favoring to its trustworthiness. Favor and disgrace are equally fear-inducing. Being ego-identified is a source of great trouble for our Human Soul. Spirit-identifying human beings are not identified with an ego-self, are identified with/ *as* a Spirit-Self and are valuing and loving all human beings as embodied Spirit and living Human Souls and can be trusted by them and entrusted with them.

MEDITATIVE INQUIRY ❖ 13

As journeying Souls, can we:

Experience that the ego's apparently positive and negative experiences, e.g., favor and disgrace, are really two equivalent sides of one coin that often is randomly flipped in life and that favor can quickly turn into disgrace at the next flip of the coin?

Experience that being totally identified with our body-ego and ego-mind and excluding Spirit and our Human Soul is only one side of an unflipped coin?

Include, unite and transcend both positive and negative dualities; disidentify from ego; connect with, value, empathize with and love all fellow human beings *as* embodied Spirit and Human Souls and open the way to living a fearless, untroubled, trustworthy and trusted human life *as* Spirit and a Human Soul?

TRANSFORMATIVE PASSAGE 14

INEFFABILITY TO EFFICACY

❖

Looking for Spirit, we are not seeing it
It is invisible, colorless
Listening for Spirit, we are not hearing it
It is inaudible, soundless
Reaching for Spirit, we are not touching it
It is intangible, formless

These three are beyond our ego's experiencing
And are merging into Spirit's Oneness

Spirit's height is not light
Spirit's depth is not dark
Continuously, endlessly
Unnamable Spirit is cycling on
Returning to No-thingness

Spirit is this formless form, imageless image
Abstruse, obscure, subtle, elusive
Confronting it, we are seeing no beginning
Following it, we are seeing no ending

We are internalizing ancient Spirit
Regulating present circumstances
Embodying primal originating
This tapestry of Spirit's Soul

EXPLICATIVE SUMMARY ❖ 14

This passage is from our Human Soul's nonmaterial, original and essential ineffability to its embodied, existential and regulatory efficacy. Spirit is a transphenomenal and ineffable Oneness, beyond ego-experiencing and describing, and our Human Soul is its uniquely embodied, internalized, individualized and efficacious personification in/*as* our essential Being, true Nature and real Self. Spirit-identified human beings are identified with the original, transphenomenal and regulatory reality of Spirit *as* the precisely woven, richly textured and vividly colored tapestry of their Human Soul.

MEDITATIVE INQUIRY ❖ 14

As journeying Souls, can we:

Identify with/*as* ancient Spirit and unify and integrate its invisibility, inaudibility and intangibility beyond the ego-limits of space-time?

Embody, internalize, assimilate, personify and enact the no-thingness, formlessness and imagelessness of Spirit and its originating, cycling and returning in/*as* our Human Soul?

Openly and fully connect with the Virtuosity, efficacious power and innate genius of our inner Spirit-nature, our Human Soul; organize, regulate and harmonize ourselves and our circumstances and actualize our individual place and contribute our unique part in the larger communal world of Human Souls and the cosmic Universe of Spirit?

TRANSFORMATIVE PASSAGE 15

IDENTIFYING TO MODERATING

❖

As ancient Spirit-Masters, we are:
Subtly mysterious, profoundly identified
Too deep to be experienced
Beyond ordinary understanding
Only described approximately

We are being:
Careful, as crossing frozen streams
Watchful, as attending to all sides
Respectful, as visiting guests
Yielding, as melting ice
Natural, as unhewn wood
Open, as spacious valleys
Undifferentiated, as muddy waters

We are purifying muddy waters
Through Spirit's serenity
We are vivifying still waters
Through Soul's fluidity

We are embodying Spirit
And not filling to overflowing
Not overflowing
There is no spilling and refilling

EXPLICATIVE SUMMARY ❖ 15

This passage is from our Human Soul's Spiritual identifications to its economical moderation. Spirit's serenity is purifying the muddy waters of ego-mind and Soul's fluidity is vivifying the stillness of ego-body. Ancient Spirit-Masters and Spirit-identifying human beings are embodying and identified with/*as* the Mystery, profundity, subtlety and transphenomenality of Spirit; are careful, watchful, respectful, yielding, natural, open and undifferentiated and can easily balance and appropriately navigate the many, rich and varied bipolarities of their embodied Soul-journeying without exceeding their Human Soul's natural limits.

MEDITATIVE INQUIRY ❖ 15

As journeying Souls, can we:

In our Soul-working and Soul-making as embodied Spirit; be careful, watchful, respectful, yielding, natural, open and undifferentiated?

Allow the myriad phenomena of our human existence and experience to naturally polarize, compensate, equalize, harmonize and centralize without soullessly engaging in artificial, unnatural, unnecessary, excessive and interfering behaviors and activities?

Embody Spirit and equalize the many bipolar phenomena of our human existence and experience without exceeding our Human Soul's natural and appropriate capacities and limits?

TRANSFORMATIVE PASSAGE 16

CONSTANCY TO SAFETY

❖

Attaining complete emptiness
Maintaining constant stillness
We are witnessing all beings
Coming into existence and cyclically returning
All beings are flourishing in living
Each one returning to Spirit's Root-Source

Returning to Spirit's Root-Source is tranquility
Tranquility is returning to Original nature
Returning to Originality is eternal Constancy

Embodying Constancy is being illuminated
Ignoring Constancy is inviting disaster

Embodying Constancy is being all-embracing
Being all-embracing is being impartial
Being impartial is being universal
Being universal is being natural
Being natural is being in accord with Spirit
According with Spirit is being everlasting
Free from endangering throughout the lifetime
Of our Human Soul

EXPLICATIVE SUMMARY ❖ 16

This passage is from our Human Soul's Spiritual Originality and Constancy to its Spiritual accord and safety. Constantly attaining, maintaining and sustaining a still body, empty heart and clear mind are embodying the tranquility, vacuity and luminosity of Spirit; pre-conditions for objectively witnessing the originating, progressing and returning of all fellow human beings and Human Souls out from and back into the Root-Source of Spirit. Spirit-identifying human beings are tranquil, original, constant, illuminated, all-embracing, impartial, universal, natural, according with Spirit, everlasting and safe.

MEDITATIVE INQUIRY ❖ 16

As journeying Souls, can we:
Be empty and still; behold and witness the birthing, living and returning of fellow human beings to the Original, Constant and Eternal Root-Source of Spirit, our inborn Spirit-nature and Human Soul, and be Soulfully illuminated and tranquil?

Experience our Human Soul as being all-embracing, impartial, universal, according with Spirit, everlasting and safe and free from being harmed by or endangering fellow human beings throughout the lifetime of our Soul-work, Soul-making and Soul-journeying?

TRANSFORMATIVE PASSAGE 17

DISTRUST TO NATURALNESS

❖

Most developed Soul-regulating
Is barely being known by people's egos
Next is being loved and praised
Next is being feared
Least developed Soul-governing
Is being despised

When we are not trusting others
Then others are not trusting us

We are minimizing words
We are completing works
And ego-identified people are saying
Everything is happening naturally
Or that we are doing it by ourselves

EXPLICATIVE SUMMARY ❖ 17

This passage is from our Human Soul's distrusting of being governed to owning the naturalness of its being, doing and living. As human beings, when we are not experiencing and exercising the personal power of our Human Soul to regulate ourselves and to organize our world; ego-identified people often take over, control and direct us. Spirit-identifying leaders are trusting and trustworthy and low-profile and quiet and are neither loved, praised nor feared by fellow human beings whose self-determination, self-regulation and self-ownership are Soulfully experienced as being natural and autonomous.

MEDITATIVE INQUIRY ❖ 17

As journeyng Souls, can we:

When in leadership positions and roles, be relatively low-profile and low-key minimalists who are non-authoritarian and non-interfering and who do not invoke either love or praise or fear and disdain in fellow human beings?

Conduct ourselves and complete our Soul-work without needs for recognition, without distrusting fellow human beings and without creating obstacles and hindrances to the natural self-determination, self-regulation and self-ownership involved in their Soul-work and Soul-making?

Provide a Spiritual context and Soulfully create optimal conditions that foster experiences of independence and autonomy and confidence and competency in fellow human beings that free and allow them to live their lives and to conduct their Soul-work and Soul-making as a natural occurrence?

TRANSFORMATIVE PASSAGE 18

FORGETTING TO REMEMBERING

❖

When we are forgetting Great Spirit
Benevolence and righteousness are appearing

When we are professing doctrines
Great hypocrisies and true believers are appearing

When we are dehumanizing families
Dutiful parents and obedient children are appearing

When we are corrupting countries
Loyal officials and patriotic citizens are appearing

EXLPLICATIVE SUMMARY ❖ 18

This passage is from our Human Soul's forgetting to remembering Great Spirit and its innate and inner Spirit-nature. Spirit-identifying human beings have not forgotten Great Spirit and lost touch with their inborn and inner Spirit-nature, Heart-of-Hearts and Human Soul and have not soullessly degenerated and devolved into being benevolent and righteous, professing doctrines, dehumanizing families and corrupting countries and becoming moralists, reformers, hypocrits, obligees and co-conspirators.

MEDITATIVE INQUIRY ❖ 18

As journeying Souls, can we:

Not forget Great Spirit by being societal 'do-gooders' and 'be-righters' who are invested in and attached to being benevolent and righteous in ego-centric and self-centered ways that are not really beneficial or truly correct?

Not soullessly profess doctrines that are untrue, spiritless dogmas and only create hypocricies and a following of fanatic true believers?

Not soullessly dehumanize families that then become unreal, loveless arrangements and only create dutiful parents and obedient children?

Not soullessly corrupt countries that then become inauthentic, heartless monoliths and only create loyal officials and patriotic citizens?

Utilize the unfortunate forgetting, degrading and disintegrating of Spirit as a fortunate opportunity to remember its Reality, purity, wholeness and greatness and to reaffirm the actuality, truth and radiant vitality, beauty and grace of our Human Hearts and Souls?

T'IEN	TI
天	地

SKY/FIRMAMENT	EARTH/SOIL
MATERIAL HEAVENS	GROUND/LAND
HEAVEN/CELESTIAL	EARTH/TERRESTRIAL
INFINITE/ETERNAL	FINITE/TEMPORAL
VAST SPACE	LOCAL PLACE
CANOPY/COVER	FOUNDATION/SUPPORT
SURROUND/ABOVE	DEPTH/BELOW
ANTHROPOMORPHIC DIETY	CIRCUMSTANCE/SITUATION
YANG CH'I/AIR/FIRE	YIN CH'I/EARTH/WATER
NATURE (WITH EARTH)	NATURE (WITH HEAVEN)

GREAT HUMAN BEINGS LIVING BETWEEN/INTEGRATING/
MEDIATING SKY AND SOIL/HEAVEN-EARTH WHICH IS NATURE,
THEIR INTEGRAL PLACE/SPACE/SITUATION/CIRCUMSTANCE.

TRANSFORMATIVE PASSAGE 19

RELINQUISHING TO SIMPLICITY

❖

As ego-identified people:
Abandoning dogmatizing and pontificating
We are benefiting one hundred fold
Relinquishing benevolence and righteousness
We are returning to being naturally loving
Eliminating craftiness and profiteering
We are discontinuing clever thievery

These three measures are external ones

As ego-identified people, let us be:
Discerning plainness
Embodying simplicity
Reducing selfishness
Diminishing desiring

EXPLICATIVE SUMMARY ❖ 19

This passage is from our Human Soul's abandoning, relinquishing and eliminating ego-motivated dogmatizing, pontificating, benevolence, righteousness, craftiness and profiteering to its living unselfishly, desirelessly, plainly and simply. The life-long journeying of our Human Soul from the derived complexities of ego to the original simplicity of Spirit involves relinquishing. Spirit-identifying human beings are not soullessly being dogmatic and pompous, benevolent and righteous and clever and crafty and are being naturally loving and Soulfully living simply and sufficiently.

MEDITATIVE INQUIRY ❖ 19

As journeying Souls, can we:

Abandon, relinquish and eliminate being intellectualized, dogmatic and preachy; falsely 'good' and rigidly 'right'; soullessly clever and crafty and exploitative and profiteering?

Live an inSpirited and enSouled human life of plainness and simplicity, egolessness and desirelessness, truthfulness and genuineness, natural loving and relating and beneficial working and serving?

TRANSFORMATIVE PASSAGE 20

RELINQUISHING TO NOURISHING

❖

Relinquishing learnedness and propriety
There is no regretting
How different are yes and yeh?
How similar are good and bad?

What ego-identified people are fearing
Must I be fearing?
How ridiculous!

Ego-identifed people are being happy
Feasting at festive banquets
Climbing up flowery terraces
I alone am unmoving, showing no signs
Like an infant, not yet imitating
Downcast, like a homeless vagrant

Ego-identified people are having plenty
I alone am lacking everything
Mine is the heart-mind of a fool
Muddled and bewildered

Ego-identified people are being bright
I alone am being dark
Ego-identified people are being sharp
I alone am being dull

Ego-identified people are making plans
I alone am being goalless
Drifting as the boundless sea
Aimless as the limitless wind

I alone am differing from ego-identified people
In drawing nourishment from Mother Spirit

EXPLICATIVE SUMMARY ❖ 20

This passage is from our Human Soul's relinquishing learnedness and propriety to its being nourished by Mother Spirit. Relinquishing, in addition to leading us to the simplicity and sufficiency of Spirit and a Soulful human life, culminates in the realization that, as human beings and Human Souls, we are essentially and completely nourished by Great Mother Spirit. Vis-a-vis the collective ethos of the societal mainstream, Spirit-identifying human beings can overtly appear to be relatively unlearned, peculiar, downcast, lacking, bewildered, dull and aimless.

MEDITATIVE INQUIRY ❖ 20

As journeying Souls, can we:
Relinquish the pretense of learnedness; the exercise of propriety, collective values and conventional behaviors and the festive and opulent lifestyles and amusements of bright and sharp ego-identified people?

Accept being different from the masses of ego-identified people without feeling strange, deficient and alone in a bustling social world where apparently happy people are busily engaged in planned undertakings and entertaining activities?

Accept appearing to be living a life of comparatively dull obscurity, foolish bewilderment and aimless drifting while being an evolved and courageous Human Soul deeply and fully nourished by Great Mother Spirit?

TRANSFORMATIVE PASSAGE 21

ELUSIVENESS TO ORIGINATING

❖

The intrinsic nature of Great Soul
Is uniquely individualizing Spirit alone

Spirit is indistinct, elusive
Elusive, indistinct
Yet within it are images
Indistinct, elusive
Yet within it are beings
Deep and dark
Within it are energies
Vital and efficacious

From ancient times until right now
Spirit's name is constantly reappearing
By which we are witnessing
The originating of all beings

How can all beginnings be experienced?
Through and as *'This'*/Spirit

Explicative Summary ❖ 21

This passage is from the elusiveness of our Human Soul's Spirit to its originating of all beings. The intrinsic nature and essential greatness of our Human Soul is its uniquely individualizing, embodying and personifying the indistinct and elusive originating Spirit. Spirit-identified and Soulful human beings are individualizing, embodying, personifying and identifying with/*as* Spirit as the Origin and beginnings of all beings as experienced in the here-now reality and actualities of their ordinary and everyday lives.

Meditative Inquiry ❖ 21

As journeying Souls, can we:

Identify with/*as* Spirit and its subtle fleeting images, deep dark beings and vital efficacious energies and witness the Spiritual Origin and Soulful originating of everyone and everything?

Experience that Spirit and our Human Soul are All That Is/As It Is/Everywhere At Once/Here And Now; the direct, concrete and immediate experiencing of just/All 'This'?

TRANSFORMATIVE PASSAGE 22

CYCLING TO RETURNING

❖

Cycling, completing
Bending, straightening
Emptying, fulfilling
Exhausting, renewing

Having little, obtaining more
Having much, becoming confused

As Spirit-identifying human beings, we are:
Embodying One
And being world models
Not displaying and are shining
Not asserting and are attracting
Not boasting and are receiving
Not parading and are enduring
Not contending with anyone
And no one is contending with us

This ancient saying:
Cycling, becoming complete
No idle words
Being complete is re-turning

EXPLICATIVE SUMMARY ❖ 22

This passage is from our Human Soul's ongoing cycling to its complete returning. Our living process and Soul-journeying are constantly, continuously and continually changing and transforming, proceeding and progressing and completing and renewing in bipolar reciprocatings, effortless flowings, seamless transitionings and cyclical returnings from the originating of life and birth, through the coursing and unfolding of growth and decline to the completing of death and rebirth. Spirit-identifying human beings are embodying the Oneness of Spirit and are being Soulfully radiant, attractive, receptive, enduring and peaceful world models by not soullessly displaying, asserting, boasting, parading and contending.

MEDITATIVE INQUIRY ❖ 22

As journeying Souls, can we:

Experience the many natural bipolarities, compensations and paradoxes that continually occur along the way of the cyclical returning of the being and living of our Human Soul to original, nondual and integral Spirit?

Embody the reality of One Spirit and be world models facilitating the journeying of our radiant, magnetic, receptive and enduring Human Soul by not egotistically asserting and displaying our power, boasting about and parading our accomplishments or conflicting and contending with fellow human beings?

Experience and fully participate in our small precious arc in the Spirit's Great Circle of Life and in the completion and culmination of our Human Soul in/*as* its cyclical Great Return to Original Spirit?

Transformative Passage 23

Transiency to Identifying

❖

Nature's Spirit is not continually expressing itself
Hurricanes are not lasting all morning
Rainstorms are not lasting all evening

What is causing this?
Heaven-Earth's Spirit
If Heaven-Earth's Spirit is not making events last long
How can we, as people, be trying to do so?

Following Spirit is identifying with/*as* Spirit
Following Soul is identifying with/*as* Soul
Following loss is identifying with/*as* loss

Spirit is endowing whomever is becoming Spirit
Soul is empowering whomever is becoming Soul
Loss is abandoning whomever is becoming loss

When we are not trusting others
Then others are not trusting us

Explicative Summary ❖ 23

This passage is from our Human Soul's transient identification with ego to its identifying *as* Spirit. All phenomena of Spirit, Nature, Heaven-Earth and our human existence, consciousness and experience; including our precious Human Being, Self, Soul and Life; are transient and temporary. As human beings, we become and are whatever we choose to follow and identify with/as along the way of our Soul's journeying, e.g., Spirit, our Human Soul or ego-loss. Spirit-identifying human beings are identifying with/as Spirit and our Human Soul and their endowing and empowering reality and actualities.

Meditative Inquiry ❖ 23

As journeying Souls, can we:

Identify with/*as*, and be endowed and empowered by, Spirit and our Human Soul rather than be ego-identified with, and being abandoned by, loss?

Trust in and follow Spirit and the journeying of our Human Soul and the Souls of fellow human beings?

TRANSFORMATIVE PASSAGE 24

DISPLAYING TO EMBODYING

❖

As ego-identified people:
When reaching, we are not solid
When striding, we are not fluid

As ego-identified people:
When displaying, we are not shining
When asserting, we are not attracting
When boasting, we are not receiving
When parading, we are not enduring

From the standpoint of Spirit
These are excessive wasteful actions
To be avoiding

As Spirit-identifying human beings
Who are embodying Spirit
We are avoiding them

EXPLICATIVE SUMMARY ❖ 24

This passage is from our Human Soul's ego-displaying to its Spirit-embodying. As human beings, from the standpoint of Spirit, when we overextend and exceed our natural limits, we are unstable and off-balance. Many of our ego-driven and self-aggrandizing behaviors are rigid and one-sided and have negative paradoxical effects and results that eclipse Spirit and displace our Human Soul. Spirit-identifying human beings are solid, fluid, shining, attracting, receiving and enduring by not engaging in soullessly excessive and wasteful actions such as displaying, asserting, boasting and parading.

MEDITATIVE INQUIRY ❖ 24

As journeying Souls, can we:

Maintain the solidity and fluidity of our being, selves, lives and Human Souls by not seeking, stretching and striving beyond our natural capacities, abilities and limits?

Avoid displaying talents, asserting positions, boasting about achievements and parading successes and, thus, not eclipse the radiant attractiveness and not foreclose the enduring receptivity of Spirit and our Human Soul?

Embody Spirit and not deplete and dissipate the vital energies of our Human Soul by engaging in extreme, excessive, extraneous and wasteful egocentric behaviors and activities?

TRANSFORMATIVE PASSAGE 25

GREATNESS TO SPONTANEITY

❖

Here is *'This'*/Spirit
Undifferentiated and complete
Preceding the birthing of Heaven-Earth
Independent, still, empty and unchanging
All-pervading and inexhaustible
It is the Great Mother of all beings
I am calling it Spirit

Being invited to identify it
I am calling it Great
Being great is going on and on
Everflowing is being far-reaching
Going beyond is returning to Root-Source

Spirit is great
Heaven is great
Earth is great
Human Soul is great
These are the four great identities
Of our universe
And Human Soul is one of them

Human Soul is following Earth
Earth is following Heaven
Heaven is following Spirit
Spirit is following its own spontaneity

Explicative Summary ❖ 25

This passage is from the greatness of our Human Soul's Spirit to its spontaneity. Great Spirit is All That Is/As It Is/Everywhere At Once/Here And Now; the direct, concrete and immediate experiencing of just/All 'This'. Spirit-identifying human beings are identifying with/*as* the greatness of Mother Spirit and its attributes, characteristics, qualities and activities and those of Heaven-Earth and the innate Spirit-nature of fellow human beings and are spontaneously following their ways.

Meditative Inquiry ❖ 25

As journeying Souls, can we:

Identify with/*as* Great Spirit and its singularity, originality, constancy, vastness, pervasiveness, emptiness, openness, stillness, inexhaustibility and greatness?

Experience ourselves, our Human Being and our Human Soul to be as great as Great Spirit, Heaven and Earth without being ego-inflated, grandiose or arrogant?

As incarnated, embodied and personified Spirit, Human Souls and Human Beings; follow the ways of Mother Earth as She follows Heaven's Design, as it follows Spirit and its spontaneity?

TRANSFORMATIVE PASSAGE 26

DISTRACTEDNESS TO CENTEREDNESS

❖

Being heavy is the ground of lightness
Being still is the center of hastiness

As Spirit-identifying human beings
We are traveling all day
Without leaving a center of gravity

Though compelling sights are along the way
We are remaining undistracted and undisturbed
Like the lords of ten thousand chariots
Who cannot afford to be frivolous

Being too light is uprooting Spirit's supporting ground
Being too hasty is unseating Spirit's regulating center

EXPLICATIVE SUMMARY ❖ 26

This passage is from our Human Soul's ego-distractions and disturbances to its Spiritual groundedness and centeredness. The groundedness and centeredness of Spirit and our Human Soul can be uprooted and unseated by the gravitational draws and pulls of compelling attractions, amusing distractions, captivating performances and entertaining side-shows in the worldly theater of human ego-being and living along the ways of the journeying of our Human Soul. Spirit-identifying human beings are constantly, continuously and continually engaged in Soul-work, Soul-making and Soul-journeying without being distracted or disturbed and too lightly uprooting the supporting ground or too hastily unseating the regulating center of Spirit, their inner Spirit-nature and Human Soul.

MEDITATIVE INQUIRY ❖ 26

As journeying Souls, can we:
Remain grounded and centered in the Reality of Spirit and the actualities of our Human Soul amid the circumstances, draws and pulls of the outer world as well as the necessities, extremes and urgencies of our inner world?

Not be distracted, disturbed and deviated by the many investments, attachments and entanglements of our ego as it vainly and persistently attempts to deny its fictional reality and to perpetuate its illusionary viability by usurping Spirit, co-opting Deeper/Higher Self and commandeering Soul?

Not take the precious Spiritual gift of our human life too lightly or live the spacious Spiritual opportunity of our human life too hastily and risk losing the solid supporting ground and the still regulating center of Spirit, our inner Spirit-nature and Human Soul?

TRANSFORMATIVE PASSAGE 27

EXCLUDING TO VALUING

❖

As most Spiritually developed travelers
We are leaving no tracks
As most Spiritually developed speakers
We are creating no doubts
As most Spiritually developed counters
We are needing no tallies

As most Spiritually developed closers
We are using no locks
Yet doors cannot be opened
As most Spiritually developed binders
We are using no knots
Yet books cannot be untied

As Spirit-identifying human beings:
We are continually assisting all people
None are being excluded
As Spirit-identifying human beings
We are continually assisting all beings
None are being excluded
This is following Spirit's Inner Light

As developed Spirit-identifying human beings:
We are teaching sources for undeveloped ones
As undeveloped ego-identified human beings
We are learning resources for developed ones
Not valuing such teachings
Not valuing such learnings
We are foolishly deviating
Despite being educated

This is Spirit's essential Secret

EXPLICATIVE SUMMARY ❖ 27

This passage is from our Human Soul's ego-exclusiveness to its Spirit-inclusiveness. The workings of Spirit in the journeying of our Human Soul are mostly invisible, inaudible and intangible but are, nonetheless, unequivocal and undeniable, efficient and effective and complete in the moment with no need for addition, subtraction or modification. Spirit-identifying human beings are creating no outward impressions, doubts or records; have a sealed closure and binding connection with Spirit; are impartially assisting fellow human beings by following the Inner Light of Spirit and have a valued reciprocal teaching and learning relationship with them in Soul-work, Soul-making, the enSouling process and Soul-journeying.

MEDITATIVE INQUIRY ❖ 27

As journeying Souls, can we:

Soul-journey softly, silently and freely; leaving no tracks, creating no doubts and needing no records and complete our Soul-work, Soul-making and Soul-journeying with a sealed closure and binding connection with Spirit?

Follow the Inner Light of Spirit and our Human Soul and impartially assist fellow human beings in their Soul-work, Soul-making and Soul-journeying without excluding any?

Value ourselves and fellow human beings as both teaching sources and learning resources and as precious opportunities for awakening, transforming, healing and evolving; an essential Spiritual secret in Soul-working, Soul-making and the enSouling process of journeying to Spirit?

HUN

魂

DIVINE/SPIRITUAL SOUL
SPIRITUAL FACULTIES
ASCENDING TO HEAVEN
INSPIRITING BODY
ANIMATION
SPIRIT-BODY

P'O

魄

ANIMAL/PHYSICAL SOUL
SENTIENT LIFE
DESCENDING TO EARTH
EMBODYING SPIRIT
INCORPORATION
BODY-SPIRIT

HUMAN LIFE AND BEING ARE THE INTEGRATION OF
THE SPIRITUAL/HUN AND THE PHYSICAL/P'O TWIN
SOULS. THE HUN SOUL IS DESCENDED FROM HEAVEN
AND IS EMBODYING AND INCORPORATING TO FORM A
BODY-SPIRIT AND THE P'O SOUL IS ASCENDED FROM
EARTH AND IS INSPIRITING AND ANIMATING TO FORM A
SPIRIT-BODY. AT THE END OF HUMAN LIFE, THE HUN
SOUL ASCENDS BACK TO HEAVEN AND THE P'O SOUL
DESCENDS BACK TO EARTH.

TRANSFORMATIVE PASSAGE 28

KNOWING TO EMBODYING

❖

Knowing masculine
Embodying feminine
Being valleys receiving our world
Being valleys of our world
We are not straying from Eternal Soul
And are returning to this Original Spirit

Knowing light
Embodying dark
Being models guiding our world
Being models of our world
We are not deviating from Constant Soul
And are returning to this Ultimate Spirit

Knowing splendor
Embodying humility
Being streams nourishing our world
Being streams of our world
We are not departing from Abundant Soul
And are returning to this Natural Spirit

As primordial simplicity is differentiating
It is becoming discrete and concrete objects
Which, as Spirit-identifying human beings, we are utilizing
As chief instruments for developing ego-identified people

Most developed Soul-regulating is not cutting up

EXPLICATIVE SUMMARY ❖ 28

This passage is from our Human Soul's knowing masculine, light and splendor to its embodying feminine, dark and humility. Soul-journeying begins with an external knowing 'about' Spirit and ends in an inner embodying 'of' Spirit that does not stray, deviate or depart from our Eternal, Constant and Abundant Human Soul; its innate Spirit-nature, Virtuosity, unique individuality, innate genius, inherent integrity, efficacious power and radiant beauty and its returning to Original, Ultimate and Natural Spirit. Spirit-identifying human beings are not straying, deviating or departing from Eternal, Constant and Abundant Soul; are returning to Original, Ultimate and Natural Spirit and are being receiving valleys, guiding models and nourishing streams for fellow human beings in the human world.

MEDITATIVE INQUIRY ❖ 28

As journeying Souls, can we:

Know masculine and embody feminine, be receptive world valleys, not stray from our Eternal Soul and return to Original Spirit?

Know light and embody dark, be guiding world models, not deviate from our Constant Soul and return to Ultimate Spirit?

Know splendor and embody humility, be nourishing world streams, not depart from our Abundant Soul and return to Natural Spirit?

Be and live the nondual, integral, primordial reality and undifferentiated simplicity of Spirit and only use the dualistic, fractional, derived actuality and differentiated complexity of our human existence and experience as instrumental means to assist ourselves and fellow human beings in Soul-work, Soul-making, Soul-journeying, Soul-regulating and Soul-returning to Spirit?

TRANSFORMATIVE PASSAGE 29

INTERFERING TO MODERATING

❖

Desiring to take over our world
Trying to control and manipulate it
I am seeing that we cannot be succeeding
Our world is a Sacred Vessel
Not for us to be interfering with
Holding onto it is losing its Spirit
Acting upon it is ruining its Soul

Among all beings in our world
Some are leading, others are following
Some are struggling, others are relaxing
Some are growing, others are declining
Some are succeeding, others are failing

As Spirit-identifying human beings, we are avoiding
Extremes, excesses, extravagances

EXPLICATIVE SUMMARY ❖ 29

This passage is from our Human Soul's ego-interfering to its Spirit-moderating. Our Soulful world of human being, existence and experience is a Sacred Vessel of Spirit, not to be interfered with, in which we human beings are naturally unique, essentially equal, harmoniously complementary and synergistically interdependent. Spirit-identifying human beings are not trying to take over, control, manipulate, interfere with, hold onto or act upon the Sacred Vessel of our Human World and are remaining Spirit-grounded and Soul-centered within it by avoiding soullessly indulging in extremes, excesses and extravagances that result in losing its Spirit and ruining its Soul.

MEDITATIVE INQUIRY ❖ 29

As journeying Souls, can we:

Maintain and sustain the original nonduality, unity, identity, integrity and Sacredness of Spirit and our Human Soul without soullessly trying to possess, dominate, control, manipulate or interfere with them and risk ruining and losing them?

Respect, honor, accept, include and allow the natural bipolar appearances, characteristics, qualities, behaviors, activities and circumstances of fellow human beings in the world as our Soulful counterparts and Spiritual wayfaring companions?

Remain Spirit-grounded and Soul-centered in the midst of all of the many bipolarities in the world of our human being, existing and experiencing and avoid extremes, excesses and extravagances through moderation?

TRANSFORMATIVE PASSAGE 30

FORCING TO ACCORDING

❖

Using Spirit in assisting ego-identified leaders
Is not controlling our world by forcing
Using force is recoiling on its users

Where ego-forces are building
Brambles are growing
Where ego-forces are fighting
Famines are following

Achieving results and stopping is acceptable
Without forcefully dominating
Achieving results and not
Priding, boasting and parading
Achieving results as a regrettable necessity

Overdeveloping power is accelerating decay
This is not according with Spirit
What is not according with Spirit
Is quickly coming to an early ending

EXPLICATIVE SUMMARY ❖ 30

This passage is from our Human Soul's ego-forcing to its Spirit-according. The overdeveloping of power and the using of force to control fellow human beings, life circumstances and world events are not in accord with Spirit; are counterproductive, impoverishing and wasteful in Soul-work, Soul-making and Soul-journeying and backfire on their users. Spirit-identifying human beings are not achieving and accomplishing by soullessly being powerful, forceful and dominating and, if successful, are not priding, boasting or parading. They are not overdeveloping power to achieve and accomplish certain objectives and, thus, are not accelerating the rapid and early ending of Soul-work, Soul-making and Soul-journeying.

MEDITATIVE INQUIRY ❖ 30

As journeying Souls, can we:

Make products, produce effects, obtain results and achieve ends, as at times regrettable necessities, without soullessly dominating fellow human beings, forcing natural processes and pridefully parading any successes?

Identify with/*as* Spirit and allow Soul-work to unfold, proceed, develop and complete itself naturally without the thorny entanglements and inevitable impoverishments that follow from using force to control or fight fellow human beings?

Not overdevelop power simply in order to achieve certain egocentric objectives or to bring about certain advantageous changes and, thus, not accelerate the decay of Spirit and the demise of our Human Soul?

WARRING TO HONORING

❖

Weapons are instruments of disaster
As Spirit-identifying human beings
We are deploring them and their use
Embodying Spirit, we are living without them

As ego-identified leaders, we are:
Honoring the left side at home
Honoring the right side at war

Weapons are instruments of disaster
As Spirit-identifying leaders
If required to use them
It is as a last resort
And with utmost restraint

Even if victorious
As Spirit-identifying leaders
We are not enjoying it
Enjoying victory is enjoying slaughtering
Enjoying slaughtering
We are not succeeding in our world

We are honoring:
The left side at fortunate events
The right side at unfortunate events
Under generals are standing on the left
Chief generals are standing on the right
An arrangement like that of a funeral

Slaughtering multitudes
Is bringing sorrow and grief
We are treating victories as funerals

EXPLICATIVE SUMMARY ❖ 31

This passage is from our Human Spirit's ego-warring to its Spirit-honoring. Even the required or restrained using of weapons to fight wars perceived as necessary or unavoidable still involves the slaughtering of fellow human beings and is a soulless deplorable disaster and grievous tragedy contrary to the reality of Spirit and the viability of our Human Soul. Spirit-identifying human beings do not use weapons to kill fellow Human Beings and Human Souls and they mourn the Human Lives, Human Selves and Human Souls lost in wars.

MEDITATIVE INQUIRY ❖ 31

As journeying Souls, can we:

Embody Spirit and live completely without needing and using weapons of war to soullessly wound, maim, kill and slaughter fellow Human Beings, Human Selves and Human Souls?

As a deeply regrettable necessity in defensive wars perceived as unavoidable, only use weapons as a last resort and with utmost restraint?

Even if victorious in war, not enjoy or celebrate the victory and, instead, treat it as an unfortunate and tragic disaster, honor our fellow Human Souls who have perished, grieve their loss and cherish and pray for peace at home?

TRANSFORMATIVE PASSAGE 32

DIFFERENTIATING TO HOMING

❖

Spirit is constant and unnamable
Although simple and subtle
No one in our world is mastering it
As Spirit-identifying leaders, when embodying it
All beings are according spontaneously

Heaven-Earth's Spirit is harmonizing
Gently raining down sweet dew
Which, without commanding,
Is falling naturally and equally
Upon all beings and Souls

Once Primordial Simplicity is differentiating
Classifying names are proliferating
Is it not time to stop?
Knowing when to stop
Is freeing us from endangering

All beings and Souls in our world
Are coming home to Spirit
Like mountain valley streams
Are flowing into the sea

EXPLICATIVE SUMMARY ❖ 32

This passage is from our Human Soul's ego-differentiating of Primordial Simplicity to its homing Returning to Spirit. Spirit is constant, subtle and simple yet difficult to nominally define or directly experience, even when we are identifying ourselves as Human Souls. Spirit-identifying human beings are embodying the ineffable Constancy, primordial Simplicity and impartial Equality of Spirit that are naturally and spontaneously Spiritually transforming, harmonizing and homing their Human Soul in its Soul-work, Soul-making and Soul-journeying.

MEDITATIVE INQUIRY ❖ 32

As journeying Souls, can we:

Embody, internalize, assimilate, personify and enact Spirit and, by our Soulful presence alone, spontaneously transform and harmonize our surroundings and fellow human beings and Human Souls?

Experience the harmony of Spirit naturally raining down the sweet dew of unity, equality, impartiality and identity upon all beings and Human Souls?

Not endanger or lose the way of Soul-journeying and become out of touch with the Ultimate Reality and Primordial Simplicity of Spirit through the exclusive making and using of analytical objectifications, intellectualized abstractions, conceptual distinctions, classifying categories, defining names and evaluative judgments?

Experience that all of us human beings, whether we know it or not, are Human Souls coming home to Spirit as naturally as mountain valley streams are flowing into the sea?

TRANSFORMATIVE PASSAGE 33

POWER TO IMMORTALITY

❖

Understanding others
We are being mentally intelligent
Understanding ourselves
We are being Spiritually illuminated

Overcoming others
We are being physically powerful
Overcoming ourselves
We are being Spiritually strong

Being content with ourselves
We are being Spiritually wealthy

Using force
We may be achieving ego-objectives
But connecting with Spirit
We are enduring

Dying without dying
We are being immortal

EXPLICATIVE SUMMARY ❖ 33

This passage is from our Human Soul's using of its ego's mental intelligence and physical power to understand and overcome fellow human beings to understanding and overcoming its ego through Spiritual illumination and strength. Understanding and overcoming fellow human beings involve intellectual knowledge and physical power but understanding and overcoming ourselves involve the Spiritual illumination and Spiritual strength that constitute Human Soul-working and Soul-making. Spirit-identifying human beings are Spiritually illuminated, strong, wealthy, connected and enduring.

MEDITATIVE INQUIRY ❖ 33

As journeying Souls, can we:
Experience the deep contentment and abundant wealth of Spirit resulting from overcoming our ego-selves, understanding our real and true inborn Spirit-nature and living as inwardly luminous Human Souls?

Allow our ego-self to die to our Human Soul and enjoy longevity and can we identify with/*as* Infinite-Eternal Spirit and enjoy immortality?

TRANSFORMATIVE PASSAGE 34

FLOWING TO GREATNESS

❖

Great Spirit is flowing everywhere
Far to the left
Far to the right
It is giving life to all beings
And is not abandoning any

It is:
Completing and forgetting its work
Without claiming any credit
Supporting and covering all beings
Without possessing any

Asking nothing, without desiring
It is being considered small
Receiving everything, without dominating
It is being considered great

As Spirit-identifying human beings:
We are not striving for greatness
And are realizing greatness

EXPLICATIVE SUMMARY ❖ 34

This passage is from our Human Soul's flowing Spirit-energy to the greatness of its Spirit-nature. The life-giving and life-sustaining Reality and Energy of Great Spirit are flowing everywhere and available to everyone. Spirit-identifying human beings are embodying and experiencing the greatness of Spirit, are supporting and protecting fellow human beings without soullessly dominating them and are completing the greatness of their Soul-working, Soul-making and Soul-journeying naturally, freely, generously and unselfconsciously.

MEDITATIVE INQUIRY ❖ 34

As journeying Souls, can we:

Embody Spirit, support and protect fellow human beings without possessing any and complete and forget our Soul-work without claiming any credit for it?

Allow our Human Soul's insignificance by not desiring or requiring anything and accept our Human Soul's magnificence by receiving and elevating everything?

Not strive to attain greatness but, rather, experience the greatness of Spirit, our inborn Spirit-nature and our Human Soul?

TRANSFORMATIVE PASSAGE 35

ENDANGERING TO INFALLIBILITY

❖

Around Spirit-identifying human beings
Embodying the Great Image of Spirit
Our whole world is gathering

Gathering and not being endangered
Being safe, secure and at peace

Music and delicacies
Are attracting passing travelers
But what Spirit is giving forth
Is minimal and flavorless

Looking for it, it is invisible
Listening for it, it is inaudible
Yet utilizing it, it is infallible

EXPLICATIVE SUMMARY ❖ 35

This passage is from our Human Soul's endangering ego-at-tractions to its Spirit's infallibility. The whole world is magnetically attracted to Soulful human beings who are embodying and identify-ing with/*as* invisible, inaudible and infallible Spirit. Spirit-identifying human beings are safe, secure, subtle and serene and are magnetically attracting fellow human beings to be likewise.

MEDITATIVE INQUIRY ❖ 35

As journeying Souls, can we:

Embody Spirit, not endanger fellow human beings and Soulfully afford them safety, security and serenity?

Trust that what issues forth from Spirit and our Human Being, Heart, Self and Soul; while invisible, inaudible, intangible and devoid of ego-flash, are of inestimable worth and infallible use in Soul-work, Soul-making and Soul-journeying?

TRANSFORMATIVE PASSAGE 36

OVERDOING TO ILLUMINATING

❖

Shrinking is following expanding
Weakening is following strengthening
Abandoning is following promoting
Depriving is following indulging
This is Soul's subtle illuminating

Tender and gentle
Are overcoming
Hard and rough

Fish are not leaving deep waters
We are not publically displaying
Powerful instruments of this Spirit-State

EXPLICATIVE SUMMARY ❖ 36

This passage is from our Human Soul's overdoing to its illuminating. The various phenomena of our human existence and experience reach their maximum degree or extent of manifestation and then naturally revert to their bipolar complementary counterparts. Spirit-identifying human beings are tender, gentle and not intentionally expanding, strengthening, promoting, indulging or displaying; and thus not shrinking, weakening, abandoning, depriving or popularizing; natural and illuminating Soul-working, Soul-making and Soul-journeying.

MEDITATIVE INQUIRY ❖ 36

As journeying Souls, can we:

Avoid overdoing in Soul-work by not attempting to expand, strengthen, promote or indulge anything since doing so only results in the opposite effect of shrinking, weakening, abandoning and depriving?

Not interfere with the natural unfolding, organic rhythms, progressive developing and illuminating realizations of Soul-work by manipulating or attempting to accelerate the natural timing of bipolar alternations and reversals in experience?

Experience that being tender and gentle in Soul-work naturally overcome the hardness and roughness of dysfunctional personality patterns, ego defense mechanisms and maladaptive survival strategies originally instituted to cope and deal with, e.g., early childhood abuse, wounding interpersonal relationships and traumatic life-experiences that have negatively impacted the inborn Spirit-nature and Human Soul of human beings?

Not publically display the subtle but powerful energies of Spirit that animate, activate, potentiate and illuminate deep inner Soul-work and Soul-making?

SHEN

身

BODY/TRUNK
SELF/PERSON
I/ME/ONESELF
THE WHOLE LIFETIME

SHEN

神

SPIRIT/SPIRITUAL
DIVINITY/DIETY/GOD
SOUL/MIND/GENIUS
SUPERNATURAL ENERGY

HUMAN BEING AND LIVING ARE THE LIFE-LONG SOUL-
JOURNEYING, UNFOLDING AND REVEALING OF THE
INTEGRAL PAIRING OF BODY AND SPIRIT, HEAVEN AND
EARTH AND YANG CH'I AND YIN CH'I ENERGIES; AN
EMBODYING/INCORPORATING OF SPIRIT AS A BODY-
SPIRIT AND AN INSPIRITING/ANIMATING OF THE BODY AS
A SPIRIT-BODY.

TRANSFORMATIVE PASSAGE 37

DOING TO SIMPLICITY

❖

Spirit is constantly not doing a 'thing'
Yet nothing is being left undone
As Spirit-identifying leaders
When we are embodying Spirit
All beings are transforming spontaneously

After developing naturally
If desiring is stirring again
We are quieting all
With Primordial Simplicity

Primordial Simplicity is being desireless
Being desireless is being at peace
Our world is settling of its own accord

EXPLICATIVE SUMMARY ❖ 37

This passage is from our Human Soul's ego-motivated doing to its simplicity of Spirit. Spirit, Spiritual energy and the activities of Spirit; being nonmaterial, invisible and intangible; appear to be 'doing' no-'thing', yet a great deal of Soul-work is being accomplished. Spirit-identifying human beings are embodying the Primordial Simplicity of Spirit and, by their Soulful presence alone, are being a transforming and peaceful influence upon fellow human beings and the human world.

MEDITATIVE INQUIRY ❖ 37

As journeying Souls, can we:

Identify with/*as*, embody, be channels and conduits for and enact the efficacious energies of Spirit and, by our Soulful presence alone, naturally and spontaneously potentiate transformative Soul-work in ourselves and fellow human beings?

Identify with/*as*, embody and transmit the Primordial Simplicity of Spirit and naturally calm our ego's desirings, stirrings and activities and those of fellow human beings?

Identify with/*as*, embody and transmit the desirelessness and peacefulness of Spirit and allow fellow human beings and the social world to settle of their own accord?

TRANSFORMATIVE PASSAGE **38**

ACTING TO INTERNALIZING

❖

Most developed Soul is not displaying Soul
And so is being the highest Soul
Least developed Soul is displaying Soul
And so is being the lowest Soul

As Spirit-identifying human beings of highest Soul
We are not acting nor having needs to be doing
As ego-identified people of lowest Soul
We are acting and having needs to be doing

As ego-identified people of most developed benevolence
We are acting but not having needs to be doing
As ego-identified people of most developed righteousness
We are acting and having needs to be doing
As ego-identified people of most developed propriety
We are acting and even forcing responses

When we are losing Spirit, Soul is appearing
When we are losing Soul, benevolence is appearing
When we are losing benevolence, righteousness is appearing
When we are losing righteousness, propriety is appearing
Now, propriety is only the superficial veneer
Of real loyalty and true fidelity
And the beginning of disaster

Foreknowledge is only an ornamental flowering of Spirit
And the beginning of ignorance

As most developed Spirit-identifying human beings, we are:
Dwelling in kernal not husk
Dwelling in fruit not flower
Rejecting the outer '*that*'/ego
Accepting the inner '*This*'/Spirit

EXPLICATIVE SUMMARY ❖ 38

This passage is from our Human Soul's ego-needful acting to its internalizing of Spirit. The most developed Human Souls do not lose their embodied identification with/*as* Spirit by being benevolent, righteous and proper and do not demonstrate or display the Soulfulness of their Spirit-nature by needing to be 'doing' any particular 'thing' or to be acting in any particular way. Spirit-identifying human beings are accepting of, and residing in, their inner-centered Spirit-nature and not in their outer-directed ego-nature or that of fellow human beings.

MEDITATIVE INQUIRY ❖ 38

As journeying Souls, can we:

Conduct our Soul-work and develop our Human Souls without egocentrically or egotistically acting in any particular way or needing to be 'doing' any particular 'thing'?

Maintain and sustain our identification with/*as* embodied Spirit and not allow it to degenerate or to displace and lose it by having ego-invested, ego-attached, ego-motivated and ego-driven needs for displaying acts of benevolence, righteousness and propriety?

Live a life of real loyalty, true fidelity and authentic commitment to being of essential, appropriate and correct benefit to fellow human beings as Soul-journeying companions?

Dwell in the deep inner fruitful Heart of the Ultimate Reality of Spirit and the Intimate Actuality of our Human Soul and not become lost in the superficial outer flowery veneer of the fictional and illusionary ego?

TRANSFORMATIVE PASSAGE 39

SEPARATENESS TO ONENESS

❖

Since ancient times, these are being One Spirit
Being the Oneness of Spirit:
Heaven is being clear
Earth is being stable
Spirit is being Sacred
Valleys are being fertile
All beings are being alive
Leaders are being Soulful
All are being so through being One Spirit

Not being clear, Heaven is cracking
Not being stable, Earth is quaking
Not being Sacred, Spirit is desisting
Not being fertile, valleys are drying up
Not being alive, all beings are dying out
Not being Soulful, leaders are falling

Great is having its foundation in humble
High is having its foundation in low
As Spirit-identifying leaders, we are calling ourselves
Orphaned, widowed and destitute
Is not this being rooted in humility?

The most praiseworthy Human Souls
Do not need or desire praise
We are not clinking like precious jade
We are not clunking like ordinary rock

EXPLICATIVE SUMMARY ❖ 39

This passage is from our Human Soul's separateness to its Spirit's Oneness. All apparently separate realities, entities, beings and human beings are animated, vitalized, energized and unified through and *as* One Spirit. Spirit-identifying human beings are one with the Oneness of Spirit and are stable, clear, Sacred, creative, energetic, Soulful, humble and modest in their Spirit-nature and Soul-journeying.

MEDITATIVE INQUIRY ❖ 39

As journeying Souls, can we:

Maintain, sustain and retain our physical stability, mental clarity, Sacred identity, creative fertility, energetic vitality and Soulfulness through identifying with/*as* One Spirit?

Humbly consider ourselves orphaned, widowed and destitute and, instead, parented by, wedded to and enriched by One Spirit?

Experience not needing or desiring praise on the praiseworthy Soulful way to One Spirit and not being either too ordinary or too precious in our inborn Spirit-nature, Soul-work, Soul-making and Soul-journeying?

Transformative Passage 40

Non-Being to All Beings

❖

Reversing and returning are the moving of Spirit
Softening and yielding are the operating of Spirit

All beings are arising from the Being of Spirit
Being is emerging from the Non-Being of Spirit

EXPLICATIVE SUMMARY ❖ 40

This passage is from our Human Soul's Spiritual Non-Being to the '10,000 things' of its Soulful experiencing. The moving and operating of the Non-Being and Being of Spirit are reversing and returning and softening and yielding. Spirit-identifying human beings are Spirit-like in the soft and yielding operating and in the reversing and returning moving of their Yin/Yang Ch'i and Wu Wei Ch'i energies.

MEDITATIVE INQUIRY ❖ 40

As journeying Souls, can we:

Maintain, sustain and retain our identification with/*as* Spirit while softening and yielding to the actualities, necessities, requirements and challenges of our lives, relationships, circumstances, activities and the many rich, diverse and varied experiences in our Soul-working, Soul-making and Soul-journeying?

Experience ourselves and fellow human beings, Soulfully, as Miraculously arising from and cyclically reverting and returning to the Mysterious Non-Being and No-thingness of Original Spirit through the natural moving and operating of Yin/Yang Ch'i and Wu Wei Ch'i energies?[9]

TRANSFORMATIVE PASSAGE 41

LAUGHABLE TO PARADOXICAL

❖

As Soul-identified human beings hearing of Spirit
We are practicing it wholeheartedly
As average human beings hearing of Spirit
We are remembering and forgetting it
As ego-identified people hearing of Spirit
We are laughing loudly at it
If we are not laughing at it
It would not be Spirit

Here is an ancient saying:
Bright Spirit is appearing dim
Advanced Spirit is appearing behind
Level Spirit is appearing uneven
High Soul is appearing lowly
Pure Soul is appearing murky
Vast Soul is appearing empty
Firm Soul is appearing flimsy
True substance is appearing shaky

Great shape is having no edges
Great talent is developing late
Great music is sounding faint
Great image is having no form

Spirit is being hidden and unnamable
Yet Spirit alone
Is developing and completing
Everyone and everything

EXPLICATIVE SUMMARY ❖ 41

This passage is from our Human Soul's ego-based laughableness to its Spirit-based paradoxical actualities. As human beings, we are not only what we eat, but also what we see, hear, feel, think, believe, value, do, etc.; any and all of which reflect our relative degree, extent and level of Spiritual development, commitment to Soul-work and Soul-making and understanding of the many paradoxes encountered throughout Soul-journeying. Spirit-identifying human beings are wholeheartedly cultivating and practicing the nondual Reality and paradoxical actualities of Spirit as it is invisibly and namelessly developing and completing their Soul-work, Soul-making and Soul-journeying.

MEDITATIVE INQUIRY ❖ 41

As journeying Souls, can we:

Cultivate the Reality of Spirit wholeheartedly without half-heartedly remembering and forgetting it or hard-heartedly laughing at the idea of it?

Accept, experience, understand, live and appreciate the many paradoxical realities and workings of Spirit and our Human Soul confronting us along the way of our Soul-journeying, Soul-work and Soul-making?

Experience that, while Spirit is invisible and ineffable, it is Spirit alone that is developing and completing the Soul-work and Soul-making of our Soul-journeying?

TRANSFORMATIVE PASSAGE 42

VIOLENCE TO COMPLETION

❖

Spirit is birthing One
One is birthing Two
Two is birthing Three
Three is birthing all beings

All beings are bearing dark Yin on their backs
All beings are enfolding bright Yang in their arms
Harmonizing these two vital energies
Is bringing all beings to completion

As ego-identified people, we are shunning
Being orphaned, widowed and destitute
Yet, as Spirit-identifying leaders
We are titling ourselves so

We are often gaining by losing
We are often losing by gaining

As ancient ones are teaching
So am I teaching once again
As aggressive and violent people
We are coming to violent endings
This is my essential Spiritual teaching

EXPLICATIVE SUMMARY ❖ 42

This passage is from our Human Soul's ego-based violence to its Spirit-based completion. The cosmogonic sequencing of Spirit is moving from its ultimateless Void of Non-Being to the Monad of Primordial Ch'i energy to the Dyad of Yang Ch'i and Yin Ch'i energies to the Triads of Non-Being/Yang Ch'i/Yin Ch'i and Heaven/Earth/ Human Being to the Myriad of All-Beings. Harmonizing Yin Ch'i and Yang Ch'i energies is central to completing Soul-work and Soul-making and soulless aggression and violence are the ending of both. Spirit-identifying human beings are integrating and harmonizing Yin Ch'i and Yang Ch'i vital energies; are being parented by, wedded to and enriched by Spirit; are living the many paradoxes of our human experience and are not ending their Soul-work, Soul-making and Soul-journeying, and possibly their precious human life, by being soullessly aggressive and violent people.

MEDITATIVE INQUIRY ❖ 42

As journeying Souls can we:

Harmonize the condensing and radiating vital Yin Ch'i/Yang Ch'i energies and bring our Soul-work and Soul-making and those of fellow human beings to completion?

Humbly identify ourselves as being orphaned, widowed and destitute and being parented by, wedded to and enriched by Spirit?

Experience the many paradoxes of living and realize that gains in Spiritual developing may appear to be ego-losses and that apparent ego-gains may actually be losses in Spiritual developing?

Not be soullessly aggressive and violent people but realize the ancient truth that being so ends our Soul-journeying, and possibly our precious human life, aggressively and violently?

TRANSFORMATIVE PASSAGE 43

HARDNESS TO SOFTNESS

❖

Softest beings in our world
Are overcomng hardest ones

The Non-Being of Spirit is entering
Where there is no-space

So, I am understanding
The usefulness of non-doing

Teaching without speaking
Practicing without acting
Rarely being realized
In our world

EXPLICATIVE SUMMARY ❖ 43

This passage is from our Human Soul's ego-hardness to its Spirit-softness. The softest beings and things in our world dissolve and melt away even the hardest of forms, beings and things and the Non-Being of Spirit enters even the most solid of forms, beings and things. Spirit-identifying human beings are soft, empty and non-doing; teaching without speaking and practicing without acting and are overcoming the hardest and densest being of ego-identified people.

MEDITATIVE INQUIRY ❖ 43

As journeying Souls, can we:

Experience the real power and true usefulness of the Non-Being, No-thingness, nonmateriality and formlessness of Spirit and identify with/*as* its ability to soften and enter the most hard and most solid of beings and things without 'doing' or forcing anything?

Accept and allow the silent teachings and the invisible workings of Spirit throughout our Soul-work, Soul-making and Soul-journeying in the world with fellow human beings?

TRANSFORMATIVE PASSAGE 44

DESIRING TO LIVING

❖

Fame or self, which is more near?
Wealth or life, which is more dear?
Gain or loss, which is more fear?

Desiring is costing a lot
Hoarding is losing a lot

Knowing what is enough
Is avoiding shaming
Knowing when to stop
Is avoiding endangering
And shortening our life

EXPLICATIVE SUMMARY ❖ 44

This passage is from our Human Soul's ego-desiring to its Spirit-living. In the life-long journeying of our Human Soul from ego to Spirit, what is more near and dear to us, life and self or wealth and fame? What evokes more fear, gain or loss? Spirit-identifying human beings are not making costly errors or risking significant losses in Soul-work, Soul-making and Soul-journeying by soullessly desiring, pursuing, acquiring and hoarding gain, wealth and fame. They are knowing, being and living the sufficiency of Spirit and are not endangering, diminishing or attenuating the longevity of their human life and Human Soul.

MEDITATIVE INQUIRY ❖ 44

As journeying Souls, can we:

Experience that desiring, pursuing, acquiring and hoarding material things, monetary wealth, social status, personal fame, vocational success and even Spiritual attainments can involve costly errors and risk significant losses in Soul-work and Soul-making?

Experience that being and living our inborn Spirit-nature, our Human Soul, provide real and true identity, vitality and sufficiency and that ending ego-desires for self-gain is avoiding shamefully endangering its viability and longevity?

TRANSFORMATIVE PASSAGE 45

PARADOX TO MODELING

❖

Spirit's completeness may seem incomplete
Yet its usefulness is infallible
Spirit's sufficiency may seem insufficient
Yet its usefulness is inexhaustible

Great propriety may appear bent
Great dexterity may appear inept
Great oratory may appear hesitant

Mobility is overcoming cold
Serenity is overcoming heat
Being clear and calm
Is being a model for our world

EXPLICATIVE SUMMARY ❖ 45

This passage is from our Human Soul's paradoxical actualities to its Spiritual modeling. The completeness and sufficiency of Spirit are the infallible and inexhaustible source of, and resource for, our Human Soul-work and Soul-making; yet, from the standpoint of our ego, they may externally and paradoxically appear to be incomplete and insufficient. Spirit-identifying human beings are not assessing and evaluating the Reality of Spirit and its workings and the actualities of our Human Soul and its forms by their outward appearances and are clearly and calmly modeling accepting and allowing the natural bipolar complements, compensations and paradoxes of our Human Soul's existence and experience.

MEDITATIVE INQUIRY ❖ 45

As journeying Souls, can we:

Experience that whatever is overtly judged by our egos to be incomplete, insufficient, bent, inept and hesitant may really be the completeness, sufficiency, uprightness, skillfulness and effectiveness of the Reality and workings of indwelling Spirit in our Soul-work, Soul-making and Soul-journeying and that of fellow human beings?

Accept, understand, allow and experience the various bipolar complements, compensations and paradoxes within our Human Soul's existence and experience as the natural workings of Spirit and be clear and calm models for fellow human beings in their Soul-work, Soul-making and Soul-journeying?

SHENG

聖

SACRED/HOLY/DIVINE
SAGE/SAGELY/WISE
SAINT/SAINTLY

HSIN

心

HEART-MIND
CENTER/MIDDLE/CORE
AFFECTIONS/INTENTIONS

SHENG JEN ARE SACRED/WISE HUMAN BEINGS WHO
ARE TAO/SPIRIT-GROUNDED/FOCUSED/CENTERED IN
THEIR INNERMOST/DEEPEST/CENTERMOST/TRUEST/
UTMOST HEART-OF-HEARTS AND WHO EMBODY/
PERSONIFY/IDENTIFY *AS* TAO/SPIRIT AND ITS NATURE,
QUALITIES, CHARACTERISTICS AND ACTIVITIES OF TE/
VIRTUOSITY/SOUL, YIN/YANG CH'I DYNAMICS, WU
WEI CH'I KINETICS, TZU JAN/NATURAL SPONTANEITY
AND WAN WU/PHENOMENAL TOTALITY. SHENG JEN ARE
TAO/SPIRIT-LIKE HUMAN BEINGS WHO ARE *BEING* TAO/
SPIRIT AND WHO ARE SOULFULLY LISTENING, HEARING,
UNDERSTANDING, OBEYING AND TRANSMITTING THE
SACREDNESS AND WISDOM OF TAO/SPIRIT.

TRANSFORMATIVE PASSAGE 46

WANTING TO SUFFICIENCY

❖

When Spirit is present in our world
Race horses are working in fields
When Spirit is not present in our world
War horses are breeding at shrines

No misfortune is greater
Than wanting what others have
No disaster is greater
Than wanting to have more
No calamity is greater
Than not having enough

Knowing that enough is enough
Is constantly having enough

EXPLICATIVE SUMMARY ❖ 46

This passage is from our Human Soul's ego-wanting to its Spiritual sufficiency. When Spirit is consciously present in a world of Soulful human beings, usual kinds of diverting entertainment are, instead, being used to nourish Soul-journeying. When Spirit is not consciously and Soulfully present, means of warfare are being prepared in Sacred places of Spiritual worship. Spirit-identifying human beings are living a life of the presence of Spirit within themselves and their worlds and are not suffering the soulless misfortunes, disasters and calamities of envy, greed and insufficiency.

MEDITATIVE INQUIRY ❖ 46

As journeying Souls, can we:
Experience that it is a great human tragedy in the journeying of our Human Soul from ego to Spirit for fellow human beings to feel lack, envy and greed and to want, to want to have more and to want to have what other people appear to have and to be out of touch with the available adequacy and sufficiency and accessible abundance and plenitude of Spirit?

Experience that identifying with/*as* Spirit is being All That Is/As It Is/Everywhere At Once/Here And Now and is constantly far more than adequately and sufficiently enough to be and to have?

TRANSFORMATIVE PASSAGE 47

EXTERIORITY TO INTERIORITY

❖

Without stepping out of doors
We are understanding our whole world
Without looking out of windows
We are comprehending Heaven's Spirit

The farther we are going
The less we are knowing

As Spirit-identifying human beings, we are:
Knowing without going
Seeing without looking
Finding without seeking
Completing without doing

EXPLICATIVE SUMMARY ❖ 47

This passage is from our Human Soul's exterior focus to its interior focus. Our physical world and social environment are a holographic corresponding microcosm of the macrocosmic Spirit dimension and Soul nature, e.g., as in the religious 'Heaven on Earth' and the alchemical 'As Above so Below'.[10] Spirit-identifying human beings are understanding and experiencing the macrocosmic-microcosmic correspondence of Heaven's Spirit and Earth's Soul through inwardly contemplating and reflecting upon their Reality and actualities without needing to venture into the physical and externalized ego-world. They are knowing without going, seeing without looking, finding without seeking and completing without doing in their Soul-work, Soul-making and Soul-journeying.

MEDITATIVE INQUIRY ❖ 47

As journeying Souls, can we:

Understand our whole human world and the workings of Spirit by contemplating, investigating and reflecting upon the deep inner reality and experience of our Human Soul as the mediating and integrative union of our Earthly and Heavenly Spiritual nature?

Experience that the farther out we are going into, and the more we are identifying with, the externalized ego-world, the less of real Spiritual significance and meaning we may be knowing?

Inwardly discover and internally come to experience and know Spirit and complete our Soul-work and Soul-making without necessarily outwardly going out seeking, looking for or 'doing' any 'thing' in the externalized ego-world?

TRANSFORMATIVE PASSAGE 48

INCREASING TO NON-DOING

❖

Pursuing knowledge is increasing daily
Cultivating Spirit is decreasing daily
Simplifying and simplifying
Again and again
Until we are reaching non-doing

Non-doing
Yet nothing is being left undone

Our Spiritual world is being gained
By non-interfering
When we are interfering
Our Spiritual world is being lost

EXPLICATIVE SUMMARY ❖ 48

This passage is from our Human Soul's ego-increasing to its Spirit's simplified non-doing. Cultivating Spirit along the way of our Soul-journeying involves simplifying ourselves and our lives until there is no one to be and no-'things' to know, get, have, keep or do. Spirit-identifying human beings are cultivating Spirit and their inner Soul-nature by decreasing, simplifying and reaching non-doing and are gaining and preserving their domain of Spirit and realm of Human Soul by not interfering with their natural workings.

MEDITATIVE INQUIRY ❖ 48

As journeying Souls, can we:

Let go of the ego-mind set that 'more is better', more things, more toys, more information, more money, more time, more people, more Self, more Spirit, more Soul, etc.?

Keep simplifying our lives in Soul-working and Soul-making by decreasing the knowing of irrelevant facts, the having of extraneous things and the doing of unnecessary activities and be reaching the non-doing of planned, devised and contrived; pointless, fruitless and meaningless and overly controlled, manipulated and forced actions?

Experience that not seeking or striving to add anything to ourselves and our lives and decreasing and reducing ego-motivated and overdone activities open the way to accepting, according with, allowing, yielding to and following the unfolding workings of Spirit which leave nothing undone?

Experience that Soul-working and Soul-making are facilitated and the dimension of Spirit is gained by not interfering with their natural workings?

Transformative Passage 49

Fixity to Equality

❖

As Spirit-identifying human beings:
We are not having fixed heart-minds
We are reflecting heart-minds of people

We are:
Being good with the good
Being good with the not-good
Such is the goodness of our Souls

We are:
Being trusting with the trustworthy
Being trusting with the untrustworthy
Such is the trustingness of our Souls

As Spirit-identifying human beings:
We are not having subjective viewpoints
We are harmonizing heart-minds of people

Ego-identified people are looking and listening
And as Spirit-identifying human beings
We are regarding them as our children

EXPLICATIVE SUMMARY ❖ 49

This passage is from our Human Soul's egocentric fixed heart-mind to its Spiritual impartial equality. The Reality of Spirit and the actualities of Soul-working are characterized by the goodness and trustingness of our Human Soul, our inner Spirit-nature. Spirit-identifying human beings are relating to fellow human beings universally, equally, impartially, intersubjectively, empathically and harmoniously and with the uncondition*ed* love that Soulful parents have for their children.

MEDITATIVE INQUIRY ❖ 49

As journeying Souls, can we:

Not have the fixed mind-sets, subjective viewpoints and habitual preferences of separate egos and, instead, Soulfully reflect and harmonize the collective and universal heart-minds of fellow human beings?

Trust both trustworthy human beings and untrustworthy people and be good with both good human beings and not-good people and, thus, impartially affirm the goodness and trustingness of our Human Soul, our inner Spirit-nature?

Accept and allow the attention of ego-identified people witnessing our Soul-working, Soul-making and Soul-journeying and regard them with the same unconditioned love, equality and impartiality that Soulful parents have for their own children?

TRANSFORMATIVE PASSAGE 50

ATTACHMENT TO IMMUNITY

❖

As ego-identifying people, we are:
Coming in at birth
Going out at death

Three out of ten of us are each:
Identifying with living
Identifying with dying
Moving between living and dying

How is this so?
Because of our attaching to life
Because of our striving for life

One out of ten of us is:
Not encountering
Tigers or rhinos on roads
Soldiers or weapons in wars
Within us, there is no place for
Claws of tigers
Horns of rhinos
Swords of soldiers

How is this so?
Because within us
There is no place for dying

EXPLICATIVE SUMMARY ❖ 50

This passage is from our Human Soul's emotional attachments and volitional strivings to its immunity and invulnerability. Most of us human beings are attached to and striving for life and living and are afraid of death and dying. A few of us do not share these attachments, strivings, anxieties and fears; are free of concerns about living or dying and experience an immunity and invulnerability to harm and injury. Spirit-identifying human beings are not strongly attached to and striving for life and living nor fearfully anticipating death and dying, are identified with/*as* Eternal Spirit and Immortal Soul and are experiencing an immunity and invulnerability to harm and injury.

MEDITATIVE INQUIRY ❖ 50

As journeying Souls, can we:

Not be attached to either living or dying and identify with/*as* the Reality of Eternal Spirit and Immortal Soul?

Identify with/*as* Eternal Spirit and Immortal Soul which have no place for dying in the consciousness of Spirit-like and Soulful human beings and which provide an immunity and invulnerabilty to harm and injury?

TRANSFORMATIVE PASSAGE 51

CONTROLLING TO NOURISHING

❖

Spirit is birthing all beings
Soul is nourishing all beings
Matter is forming all beings
Circumstance is completing all beings

So, all awakened beings are:
Honoring Spirit, cherishing Soul
Constantly, naturally
Without anyone commanding

Spirit is birthing all beings
Soul is nourishing all beings
Protecting and sustaining
Comforting and supporting
Fostering and developing

So, we are:
Birthing without possessing
Assisting without controlling
Guiding without forcing

This is Soul's Mysterious Virtuosity

EXPLICATIVE SUMMARY ❖ 51

This passage is from our Human Soul's ego-controlling and forcing to its nourishing Virtuosity. Spirit is the Origin of all beings; its Virtuosity, our inborn Spirit-nature and Human Soul, nourishes them; matter forms them and the circumstances of our lives complete them. Spirit-identifying human beings are naturally, constantly and freely honoring the Reality of Spirit and cherishing the Virtuosity of our Human Soul and are nourishing, protecting, sustaining, comforting, supporting, assisting, fostering, guiding and developing fellow human beings in their Soul-work, Soul-making and Soul-journeying by Soulfully embodying and enacting the Mysterious Virtuosity of Spirit without being possessive, controlling and forceful.

MEDITATIVE INQUIRY ❖ 51

As journeying Souls, can we:

Honor Spirit and cherish its Virtuosity, our inborn Spirit-nature and Human Soul, naturally and constantly without being commanded to do so?

Experience that Spirit originates all human beings and that our Human Soul, its Virtuosity; nourishes, protects, sustains, comforts, supports, assists, fosters, guides and develops us throughout the many forms, circumstances, events and experiences of our lives?

Create and materialize the conditions and circumstances that will presence, assist and guide fellow human beings in their Soul-work, Soul-making and Soul-journeying without being possessive, controlling or forcing and by Soulfully embodying and enacting the Mysterious Virtuosity of Spirit and our Human Soul?

TRANSFORMATIVE PASSAGE 52

ENDANGERING TO COMPLETING

❖

Here is the beginning of our world
Which is being called Mother Spirit
Understanding Mother Spirit
Is understanding Her offspring
Understanding Her offspring
And embracing Mother Spirit
Is being free from endangering
For our whole life

When we are:
Sealing the openings
Closing the gateways
To the ending of living
We are not endangering

When we are:
Opening the passages
Meddling with events
To the ending of living
We are not completing

Perceiving subtleness is illuminating
Embodying tenderness is strengthening
Utilizing our outer radiating
And returning to inner illuminating
We are not endangering living

This is according with Constant Spirit

EXPLICATIVE SUMMARY ❖ 52

This passage is from our Human Soul's ego-endangering to its Spiritual completing. The beginning of our human world can be experienced as Great Mother, Great Mother Spirit of Origin, Great Spirit Mother of all Human Souls. Spirit-identifying human beings are understanding and embracing Mother Spirit and fellow human beings as Her progeny and are free from endangering them and their lives. They are limiting external sensory stimulation, are not interfering with fellow human beings and world events and are not endangering the successful completing of their Soul-journeying. Spirit-identifying human beings are according with the Constancy of Great Mother Spirit and identifying with/*as* Her subtle illuminating and tender strengthening.

MEDITATIVE INQUIRY ❖ 52

As journeying Souls, can we:

Embrace Great Mother Spirit and experience all fellow human beings equally and impartially as Her offspring and be free from endangering and being endangered for our whole lifetime?

Cultivate, develop and seal our embodied Spirit and inSpirited body by limiting external sensory stimulation; not draining our Human Soul's vital life energy; not interfering with fellow human beings and not endangering our immunity, invulnerability and longevity and risking not completing our Soul-work and Soul-making?

Strengthen and illuminate our inborn Spirit-nature, our Human Soul, and safeguard our living by perceiving the subtleness and embodying the tenderness of Great Mother Spirit, inverting our radiant consciousness and according with Her constant creating and nourishing of our Spiritual family of kindred Human Souls?

TRANSFORMATIVE PASSAGE 53

DEVIATING TO CULTIVATING

❖

Having the least bit of wisdom
I am traveling Spirit's Great Pathway
Fearing only deviating

Spirit's Great Pathway is wide and direct
Yet, ego-identified people are taking detours

Courts are being overdecorated
Grounds are being uncultivated
Storehouses are being depleted

Elegant costumes are being paraded
Ornate weapons are being displayed
Fancy delicacies are being devoured
Surplus riches are being stockpiled

All of this is vanity and thievery
Certainly not cultivating Spirit

EXPLICATIVE SUMMARY ❖ 53

This passage is from our Human Soul's ego-deviating to its Spirit-cultivating. As Soul-journeyers along the way from ego to Spirit, we need only be fearing deviating and straying from the Great Pathway of Spirit. Spirit-identifying human beings are not taking short-cuts, side-tracks, by-paths and detours in their Soul-journeying; are cultivating Spirit and are not displacing their Human Soul by soullessly engaging and indulging in the distractions, deviations and diversions and the excesses, extravagances and extremes of ego-centric, ego-bound and ego-driven living.

MEDITATIVE INQUIRY ❖ 53

As journeying Souls, can we:

Wisely fear deviating and straying from the wide and direct Great Pathway of Spirit by taking short-cuts, side-tracks, by-paths and detours?

Cultivate the Ground of Spirit and not deplete our Human Soul's vital life energies by embellishing and ornamenting our egos and displacing our Human Souls by vainly and soullessly indulging fancies, hoarding riches, displaying finery and parading elegance?

Cultivate Spirit by not engaging in the deviating thievery our ego poses to Soul-working and Soul-making by its excessive needs for absorbing distractions, entrancing diversions, entertaining side-shows, spectator sports and vicarious living?

TRANSFORMATIVE PASSAGE 54

UPROOTING TO CONTEMPLATING

❖

Well-founded Spirit
Cannot be uprooted
Well-enfolded Spirit
Cannot be removed

Generation after generation
Is continuing this Soul-making

Cultivating Soul:
In ourselves is embodying Soul
In our families is compounding Soul
In our communities is enduring Soul
In our countries is abounding Soul
In our worlds is pervading Soul

Therefore, we are contemplating
Selves in light of ourselves
Families in light of our families
Communities in light of our communities
Countries in light of our countries
Worlds in light of our worlds

How am I knowing
That this is so in our world?
Through and *as 'This'*/Spirit

EXPLICATIVE SUMMARY ❖ 54

This passage is from our Human Soul's ego-uprooting to its Spiritual contemplating. Well founded and enfolded Spirit cannot be uprooted or removed and can be cultivated, compounded and radiantly suffused for the benefit of ourselves and our familiies, communities, countries and world. Spirit-identifying human beings have a well-founded and well-enfolded Spirit and an embodied, compounded, enduring, abounding and pervading Human Soul that radiantly and radially influence (creates an in-flowing) the fellow human beings with whom they are related, connected and communing.

MEDITATIVE INQUIRY ❖ 54

As journeying Souls, can we:

Solidly ground and firmly center ourselves in Spirit and its Virtuosity, our inborn Spirit-nature and Human Soul, without uprooting or severing our precious and often delicate connection with them?

Cultivate Soul, the Virtuosity of Spirit, in ourselves, our families, our communities, our countries and our worlds and experience its embodying, compounding, enduring, abounding and pervading in our Beings, Selves and Hearts as our shared inborn Spirit-nature and Human Soul?

Contemplate and connect with fellow human beings; our families, communities, countries and world, in light of Spirit and our own cultivated Human Soul and exert a beneficial radiating influence (in-flowing) upon and within them?

LING

靈

SPIRIT OF A BEING
SPIRIT/SOUL/MIND
DIVINE/DIETY
SUPERNATURAL INFLUENCE
EFFICACIOUS/EFFECTIVE

LU

路

ROAD/PATH/WAY
JOURNEY/TRAVEL
ROUTE/DISTANCE
MEANS/SEQUENCE
KIND/SORT

AS HUMAN BEINGS, OUR LIVES ARE A SPIRITUAL
WAYFARING JOURNEY THAT EACH ONE OF US IS MAKING
IN THE ABSOLUTELY UNIQUE WAY THAT WE ARE GOING
THROUGH IT; ALL BEING NOURISHED, INFLUENCED
AND CLEANSED BY THE GENTLE FALLING RAIN
OF DIVINE BLESSING AND GRACE UPON
AND WITHIN OUR HUMAN SOULS.

TRANSFORMATIVE PASSAGE 55

VULNERABILITY TO HARMONY

❖

Embodying abundant Soul
We are resembling an infant child
Poisonous insects are not stinging us
Wild animals are not attacking us
Predatory birds are not striking us

Like an infant child
Our bones are flexible
Our muscles are supple
Yet our grasp is strong

Like an infant child
Not yet knowing the uniting
Of feminine and masculine
Our life force is perfect

Like an infant child
Crying all day long
Without becoming hoarse
Our natural harmony is perfect

Being harmonious
Is according with Constant Spirit
According with Constant Spirit
Is being illuminated

Forcing the growing of life is ominous
Using our heart-mind
For manipulating our vital energy is powerful
But overdeveloping power is accelerating decay
This is not according with Spirit
What is not according with Spirit
Is quickly coming to an early ending

EXPLICATIVE SUMMARY ❖ 55

This passage is from our Human Soul's ego-vulnerability to its Spirit-harmony. Identifying with/*as* Spirit and embodying the abundant and efficacious power of its Virtuosity, our inborn Spirit-nature and Human Soul, endow human beings with longevity and an immunity and invulnerability to harm and injury. Spirit-identifying human beings are according with Constant Spirit and embodying abundant Human Soul. They are strong, flexible, vital, harmonious and illuminated and are not soullessly overdeveloping power, manipulating their Human Soul's vital energy, forcing the growing of life and accelerating the decay, deterioration and demise of Soul-work, Soul-making and Soul-journeying.

MEDITATIVE INQUIRY ❖ 55

As journeying Souls, can we:

Embody the Virtuosity of Spirit, our inborn Spirit-nature and Human Soul, and resemble the immunity, invulnerablity, flexibility, vitality and harmony of an infant child?

Accord with Constant Spirit and experience the harmony and illumination of its Virtuosity, our inborn Spirit-nature and Human Soul?

Not force the growth of ourselves, fellow human beings and all living beings by manipulating the vital energies or overdeveloping the efficacious power of our Human Soul and thus be accelerating its decay?

Not engage in unharmonious and unilluminated behaviors and activities that are not in accord with Spirit and which bring about an early ending to Soul-working, Soul-making and Soul-journeying?

TRANSFORMATIVE PASSAGE 56

COMPENSATING TO IDENTIFYING

❖

Understanding, we are not necessarily speaking
Speaking, we are not necessarily understanding

We are:
Sealing the openings
Closing the gateways
Smoothing sharp edges
Loosening tight knots
Softening bright lights
Settling dusty worlds
This is profoundly identifying
With/*as* Spirit and Soul

When we are profoundly identifying
It is impossible to be:
Intimate or indifferent with us
Helpful or harmful to us
Commending or condemning of us

As such, we are being
The greatest Spiritual treasure
Of our whole world

EXPLICATIVE SUMMARY ❖ 56

This passage is from our Human Soul's compensating to its Spirit-identifying. Human beings who have a real experience and true understanding of, and are profoundly identifying with/*as* Spirit and Human Soul; are not usually speaking about them or being the objects of the dualistic projections, affections, behaviors and judgments of fellow human beings. Spirit-identifying human beings are understanding, but not ordinarily speaking about, the Reality of Spirit and the actualities of the Human Soul and their nature and workings. They are closing themselves off from external sensory stimulation and are embodying and enacting the complementary and compensatory counterbalancing of the various bipolarities of the Human Soul's existence and experience. Spirit-identifying human beings are independent of both the intimacy, helpfulness and commendation and the indifference, harmfulness and condemnation of fellow human beings and, as such, are regarded as a great Spiritual treasure.

MEDITATIVE INQUIRY ❖ 56

As journeying Souls, can we:
Close ourselves off from external sensory stimulation, profoundly identify with/*as* Spirit and be able to naturally counterbalance and compensate the various bipolarities of our Human Soul's existence and experience, e.g., soothe pain, relax tension, soften intensity and clear confusion?

Profoundly identify with/*as* Spirit, not be exclusively and dualistically one-sided and be accepting of fellow human beings as being unable to be either intimate or indifferent with us, helpful or harmful to us or commending or condemning of us and to be regarding us as our world's greatest Spiritual treasure?

Transformative Passage 57

Interfering to Spontaneity

❖

We are regulating Spirit-States straightforwardly
We are deploying armies strategically
We are gaining our world by not interfering
How are we knowing that this is so?
Through and *as 'This'*/Spirit

More restrictions and prohibitions
More impoverished people
More machines and weapons
More disordered countries
More cleverness and craftiness
More cunning contrivances
More regulations and ordinances
More criminal activities

As Spirit-identifying human beings:
We are not forcing
People are transforming of themselves so
We are not controlling
People are regulating of themselves so
We are not interfering
People are prospering of themselves so
We are not desiring
People are simplifying of themselves so

EXPLICATIVE SUMMARY ❖ 57

This passage is from our Human Soul's ego-interfering to its Spirit's spontaneity of-itself-so. Experiencing Spirit as All That Is/ As It Is/Everywhere At Once/Here And Now demonstrates that real leadership and true governance do not involve adopting militaristic strategies but, rather, are characterized by not soullessly controlling, forcing, restricting or otherwise interfering with the natural Soulful unfolding, regulating, transforming, developing, prospering and simplifying of fellow human beings, social activities and world affairs. Spirit-identifying human beings are regulating Spirit-states straightforwardly, rather than strategically, and through harmonizing, rather than interfering. They are not being soullessly restrictive, mechanistic, crafty and legalistic and the fellow human beings with whom they are associated and involved are not impoverished, disorderly, cunning and criminal. Spirit-identifying human beings are not forcing and controlling, or invested and interfering in, the lives of fellow human beings and are allowing them to transform, regulate, enhance and simplify their lives on their own, of themselves so.

MEDITATIVE INQUIRY ❖ 57

As journeying Souls, can we:

Not employ machines and weapons that disorder our countries; not contrive clever and crafty schemes, not implement cunning and adroit strategies and not institute restrictions, prohibitions, regulations and ordinances that soullessly impoverish fellow human beings, foster criminal activities and greatly impede and impair Soul-working and Soul-making?

Not control, force, interfere with and complicate the lives of fellow human beings and, instead, allow them to naturally and spontaneously self-regulate, transform, prosper and simplify on their own, of themselves so, in their own Soul-working, Soul-making and Soul-journeying?

TRANSFORMATIVE PASSAGE 58

DOMINATING TO MODERATING

❖

When regulating is being subdued and unobtrusive
People are being encouraged and contented
When governing is being demanding and intrusive
People are being discouraged and discontented

Good fortune is resting upon bad fortune
Bad fortune is residing in good fortune
Who is knowing how and when it will be ending?
Is their neither right nor wrong?
Right is turning into wrong
Wrong is turning into right
As ego-identified people
Long have we been bewildered

As Spirit-identifying human beings, we are
Upright, yet not overbearing
Straightforward, yet not overextending
Sharp, yet not piercing
Bright, yet not dazzling

EXPLICATIVE SUMMARY ❖ 58

This passage is from our Human Soul's ego-dominating to its Spirit-moderating. Subdued and unobtrusive Soulful regulating of fellow human beings is encouraging and fosters contentment and dominating and invasive soulless governing is discouraging and engenders discontent. The sometimes paradoxical, relative and shifting nature of moral and ethical standards of what is good and bad, right and wrong, have long bewildered ego-identified people in their Soul-journeying. Spirit-identifying human beings are being Soulfully subdued, unobtrusive, encouraging, upright, straightforward, sharp and bright and are not being soullessly dominating, invasive, discouraging, overbearing, overextending, piercing and dazzling.

MEDITATIVE INQUIRY ❖ 58

As journeying Souls, can we:

In leadership roles, be low-profile, low-key, non-dominating and non-invasive and Soulfully foster encouragement and contentment in fellow human beings rather than be high-profile, high-powered, dominating and invasive and soullessly engender discouragement and discontent?

In leadership positions, be precise, clear and consistent in Soulfully defining, implementing and following through with standards of what is desirable, correct, appropriate and acceptable in organizational policies and behavioral expectations so as not to soullessly bewilder fellow human beings with inconsistencies, double standards, favoritism, loopholes and escape clauses?

In leadership behavior, relationships and actions, be Soulfully moderate, upright, straightforward, sharp and bright but not soullessly extreme, overbearing, overextending, piercing and dazzling?

TRANSFORMATIVE PASSAGE 59

CONSERVING TO LONGEVITY

❖

In serving Heaven's Spirit and Human Soul
And regulating ego-identified people
We are being sparing
Being sparing is yielding early
Yielding early is compounding Soul

Compounding Soul is overcoming anything
Overcoming anything is having unlimited capacity
Unlimited capacity is regulating any ego-state

Embracing Mother of this Spirit-State
We are being long-lasting
This is having deep roots and solid trunks
The way of long-lasting life and far-reaching vision

EXPLICATIVE SUMMARY ❖ 59

This passage is from our Human Soul's conserving energy to its longevity. Reserving, conserving, preserving and not leaking, draining and dissipating the vital energy of Spirit's Virtuosity, our inborn Spirit-nature and Human Soul, are compounding its efficacious power, resulting in unlimited capacity and the ability to regulate and overcome any ego-state and to insure a long and visionary life. Spirit-identifying human beings are serving Heaven's Spirit and their Human Soul, are being frugal and yielding, are conserving and compounding vital Soul energy and are having unlimited capacity and energy reservoirs to overcome and to regulate ego-states. They are embracing Mother-Spirit, are deeply rooted in, and solidly connected with, Spirit and are enjoying a long-lasting life and far-reaching vision in their Soul-journeying.

MEDITATIVE INQUIRY ❖ 59

As journeying Souls, can we:

As leaders, serve Spirit and the Souls of fellow human beings by conserving and not wasting our Human Soul's vital life energy in resistant and unyielding behavior, unilateral and conflicted relationships and extraneous and irrelevant activities and, thus, compound it and increase our capacity and ability to overcome ego-identifications and to Soulfully regulate states of consciousness?

Embrace and identify with/*as* Great Mother Spirit and deepen and solidify our foundation and connection with Spirit and live a long-lasting Soulful life of splendid far-reaching Spiritual revelations?

TRANSFORMATIVE PASSAGE 60

HINDERING TO BENEFITING

❖

We are regulating a great Spirit-State
As if cooking small fishes

When we are regulating our world with Spirit
Phantoms are losing supernatural powers
Not that phantoms are losing supernatural powers
But that they are no longer hindering us
Not that they are no longer hindering us
But that sages are also not hindering us

When both are not hindering us
Soul is accumulating in both
Collectively benefiting all beings
Refreshing, restoring, returning

EXPLICATIVE SUMMARY ❖ 60

This passage is from our Human Soul's ego-hindering to its Spirit-benefiting. Regulating ourselves, fellow human beings and our world by Spirit, its Virtuosity, our inborn Spirit-nature and Human Soul; is conducted attentively, gently, carefully and minimally without giving power to, or taking power from, supernatural spirit-entities and superhuman Spirit-beings, e.g., phantoms or saints. Spirit-identifying human beings are regulating Spirit-states and Soul-natures attentively, gently, carefully and minimally and are deconstituting, integrating and not being hindered by, the accorded powers of both supernatural entities and superhuman beings and, thus, are serving to accumulate and compound their Soul's energies in the consciousness of fellow human beings for their collective benefit and revitalizing.

MEDITATIVE INQUIRY ❖ 60

As journeying Souls, can we:

Regulate our Spirit-State naturally and gently without excessive handling and manipulating and by utilizing the efficacious power of Spirit's Virtuosity, our inborn Spirit-nature and Human Soul?

Disempower both superhuman incarnated beings, e.g., demigods, avatars, saints and wizards and supernatural disincarnate entities, e.g., ghosts, phantoms, spectres and apparitions, by withdrawing projections and deconstituting introjections, so that they are no longer hindering our own Soul-work, Soul-making and Soul-journeying to Spirit?

Experience that when both supernatural entities and superhuman beings are disempowered by our ego and projections withdrawn, the efficacious power and Virtuosity of Spirit accumulates in both and collectively benefits and revitalizes fellow human beings, Soul-working, Soul-making and returning to Spirit?

TRANSFORMATIVE PASSAGE 61

LOWERING TO FULFILLING

❖

Great Spirit-States are being like river deltas
They are converging points of our world
They are being the feminine of our world
Feminine is constantly overcoming masculine
By naturally being low, deep and still

Great Spirit-States are receiving small ego-states
By lowering themselves before them
Small ego-states are receiving Great Spirit-States
By lowering themselves before them
The former are receiving by consciously lowering
The latter are receiving by naturally being lower

Great Spirit-States are wanting to include and provide
Small ego-states are wanting to join and serve
Both states are obtaining what they want
By Spirit-States lowering themselves

EXPLICATIVE SUMMARY ❖ 61

This passage is from our Human Soul's lowering to its Spirit-fulfilling. As Soul-journeying human beings identifying with/*as* Spirit, our inborn Spirit-nature and Human Soul; we are being low, deep and still and, like the downward pull of gravity, are converging points for fellow human beings in the world. Spirit-identifying human beings are identifying with/*as* the Feminine Spirit; are being low, deep and still; are converging points for fellow human beings in the world and are including, supporting and providing for them in their Soul-working, Soul-making and Soul-journeying.

MEDITATIVE INQUIRY ❖ 61

As journeying Souls, can we:

Identify with/*as* the Feminine Spirit and its lowness, earthiness, deepness, downward and inward flowingness, magnetic attractiveness and centripetal receptiveness?

Humbly lower ourselves before fellow human beings, openly receive them and include and provide for them as they join us, serve Spirit and contribute to fulfilling Soul-work, Soul-making and Soul-journeying?

TRANSFORMATIVE PASSAGE 62

GIFTING TO TREASURING

❖

Spirit is being the sanctuary of all beings
As Spirit-identifying human beings
It is our perfection
As ego-identified people
It is our protection

Fine words are buying favor
Good deeds are winning over
Yet even if we are not developing
Spirit is not abandoning us

At the crowning of emperors
And the installing of ministers
Rather than presenting jade discs and horse teams
We are sitting still and humbly offering Spirit

As Ancient Spirit-identified Ones:
Why are we so treasuring Spirit?
Because seeking Spirit, we are coming to Spirit
Because not seeking Spirit, Spirit is coming to us
Thus, Spirit is being our world's greatest treasure

EXPLICATIVE SUMMARY ❖ 62

This is the passage from our Human Soul's ego-gifting to its Spirit-treasuring. Spirit is the everpresent, constant and impartial sanctuary and treasure of all human beings; the protection for, and the perfection of, our Soul-work, Soul-making and Soul-journeying. Spirit-identifying human beings are experiencing that Spirit is a sanctuary; the protection for ego-identified people and the perfection of Spirit-identifying human beings. Spirit-identifying human beings are experiencing that Constant, Infinite and Eternal Spirit is everpresent and never abandons fellow human beings regardless of their degree, extent or level of Spiritual and Soul development. They are acknowledging the progress, accomplishments and attainments of the Soul-working and Soul-making of fellow human beings by sitting still and humbly offering Spirit rather than by presenting material gifts. Spirit-identifying human beings are treasuring Spirit because seeking Spirit, we are coming to Spirit and not seeking Spirit, Spirit is coming to us.

MEDITATIVE INQUIRY ❖ 62

As journeying Souls, can we:

Experience that Spirit is a sanctuary; the perfection of Spirit-identified Human Souls and the protection for ego-identified Human Souls?

Experience that, while fine words and good deeds can temporarily buy favors from and win over people; it is Constant, Infinite and Eternal Spirit that never prefers or abandons us in our Soul-working, Soul-making and Soul-journeying?

Remain still and humbly and Soulfully offer Spirit to ego-identified people, rather than acknowledge and reward the progress, attainments and accomplishments of their Soul-working and Soul-making with material gifts?

Experience, as Ancient Spirit-identified Ones have done, that Spirit is our world's greatest treasure because all of us human beings are Soul-journeying from ego to Spirit whether or not we are seeking it or whether or not we are knowing it?

TRANSFORMATIVE PASSAGE 63

DIFFICULTY TO GREATNESS

❖

We are:
Acting without forcing
Serving without striving
Tasting without savoring

We are:
Making great small
Making many few
Repaying hurt with Soul

We are:
Addressing difficult issues early
While they are still being easy
Addressing great matters early
While they are still being small

Difficult issues are beginning with easy ones
Great matters are beginning with small ones

As Spirit-identifying human beings:
We are not striving for great accomplishments
Yet are achieving greatness
As ego-identified people who are making easy promises
We are lacking in credibility and trust
Such easiness is leading to great difficulties

As Spirit-identifying human beings:
We are considering everything difficult
And, to the end, are meeting no difficulty

EXPLICATIVE SUMMARY ❖ 63

This passage is from our Human Soul's ego-difficulty to its Spirit-greatness. Many problems, great matters and difficult issues are beginning with a few small and easy ones, if and when addressed early. Spirit-identifying human beings are tasting without savoring, acting without forcing and serving without striving; are making the great small and the many few and are repaying hurt with Soul. They are, in their Soul-journeying, addressing difficult issues and great matters early when they are still being easy and small; are not striving for great accomplishments or making easy promises; are considering everything difficult and, to the end, are meeting no difficulties.

MEDITATIVE INQUIRY ❖ 63

As journeying Souls, can we:

Enact ourselves without forcing, serve Spirit without striving and experience our Human Soul without objectifying it?

Make the greatness of Spirit small enough to embody as our Human Soul, make the multiplicity of ego-exeriences few enough to personify as our Human Soul and repay any human hurt with the Virtuosity of Spirit, our inborn Spirit-nature and Human Soul?

Begin the great matter of conscious Soul-working and Soul-making and address its often difficult issues early when they may still be relatively fewer, smaller and easier?

Not strive for great accomplishments, not deny difficult issues, not trust easy promises and, thus, open and be on the way to achieving the greatness of Spirit and a credible and trustworthy Human Soul?

Consider everything about Soul-working and Soul-making difficult and, paradoxically, to and in the end meet no difficulty?

YU

游

SWIM/FLOAT
TRAVEL/WANDER
STROLL/SAUNTER
ROAM/ROVE

PAN

伴

COMPANION
PARTNER
ASSOCIATE
KEEP COMPANY
A PAIR

P'ENG

朋

FRIEND
COMPANION
ASSOCIATE
PEER/MATCH
A PAIR

YU

友

FRIEND
COMPANION
ASSOCIATE
GROUP OF 2
A PAIR

AS HUMAN BEINGS, OUR CAREFREE WAYFARING
WANDERINGS ARE BEST ENJOYED BY BEING TOGETHER
WITH A FRIENDLY ASSOCIATE, COMPANION AND PARTNER,
ONE HALF OF A HUMAN PAIR; LIVING, EXPERIENCING
AND SHARING OUR SOULFUL JOURNEY AND SPIRITUAL
PILGRIMAGE TO AWAKENING, TRANSFORMING
AND EVOLVING.

TRANSFORMATIVE PASSAGE 64

RUINING TO DEVELOPING

❖

What is:
Still is easy to maintain
Subtle is easy to sustain
What is:
Frail is easy to shatter
Small is easy to scatter

We are anticipating issues
Before they are coming into being
We are regulating matters
Before they are going out of order

Large trees are growing from tiny shoots
Tall towers are rising from small mounds
Long trips are starting from first steps

Forcing is ruining
Seizing is losing
As Spirit-identifying human beings, we are:
Forcing nothing and ruining nothing
Seizing nothing and losing nothing

As ego-identified people, we are often failing
When close to completing
When we are being as attentive
At endings as we are at beginnings
Nothing is being ruined or lost

As Spirit-identifying human beings, we are:
Desiring to be desireless
Not valuing rare objects
Learning to be unlearned
Returning to what people are disregarding
Assisting all beings to develop naturally
Without ourselves acting unnaturally

Explicative Summary ❖ 64

This passage is from our Human Soul's ego-ruining to its natural Spiritual developing. Whatever is still and subtle is easy to maintain and sustain and whatever is frail and small is easy to shatter and scatter. Large trees are growing from tiny shoots, tall towers are rising from small mounds and long journeys are beginning from first steps. Spirit-identifying human beings are anticipating and regulating issues and matters before they are coming into being or going out of order. They are forcing nothing and ruining nothing and are seizing nothing and are losing nothing and, when close to completing things, are as attentive at their ending as they were at their beginning. Spirit-identifying human beings are desiring to be desireless, are not valuing rare objects, are learning to be unlearned, are returning to the Spirit that many fellow human beings are disregarding and are assisting them in developing their Human Souls naturally without themselves acting unnaturally.

Meditative Inquiry ❖ 64

As journeying Souls, can we:

Anticipate issues and regulate matters in our Soul-working and Soul-making before they are coming into being or going out of order?

Appreciate that the great life-long journeying of our Human Soul to becoming and being an embodied Spirit/body-Spirit and an inSpirited body/Spirit-body began from our little ego-self?

Not force the natural unfolding and developing of our Human Soul or seize onto its transient manifesting and progressing and risk ruining or losing its completing?

Be as attentive near the endings of developments in our Soul-work, Soul-making and Soul-journeying as we are at their still, subtle, small and fragile beginnings so as not to ruin, lose or fail to complete them?

Throughout the developing and completing of Soul-working, Soul-making and Soul-journeying; desire to be desireless, learn to be unlearned, return to Spirit and assist fellow human beings in developing their Human Soul naturally without ourselves acting unnaturally?

TRANSFORMATIVE PASSAGE 65

CLEVERNESS TO CLEARNESS

❖

Being Ancient Ones fully identified with/*as* Spirit
We are not using it for enlightening people
But rather for restoring Primordial Simplicity

As ego-identified people
We are difficult to govern
Because of being too sophisticated

Clever governing is ruining this Spirit-State
Clear regulating is blessing this Spirit-State
Understanding these two matters
We are understanding Spirit's Principle
Constantly embodying Spirit's Principle
Is Spirit's Profound Virtuosity

Spirit's Profound Virtuosity
Is deeply penetrating and far-reaching
Returning all beings to the Original Spirit-State
Reaching all the way back to its Complete Harmony

EXPLICATIVE SUMMARY ❖ 65

This passage is from our Human Soul's ego-cleverness to its Spiritual clearness. The Profound Virtuosity of Spirit, our inborn Spirit-nature and Human Soul, is deeply penetrating, far-reaching and returning all human beings to the original Unity, Identity, Totality and Harmony of Spirit. Spirit-identifying human beings are clearly regulating Spirit-states without cleverness; are restoring the Primordial Simplicity of, rather than enlightening, fellow human beings; are embodying and enacting the ancient Principle of Spirit and its deeply penetrating and far-reaching Profound Virtuosity and are assisting fellow human beings in returning to the Original Spirit-State and its Complete Harmony.

MEDITATIVE INQUIRY ❖ 65

As journeying Souls, can we:

Like Ancient ones, be fully identified with/*as* Spirit and not be using it to enlighten or add to the oversophistication of ego-identified people but, rather, to restore the Primordial Simplicity of their Original Spirit and deep Human Soul?

Embody Spirit and its profound Virtuosity, our inborn Spirit-nature and Human Soul, by constantly understanding and experiencing that the clear regulating of Soul-journeying is Soulfully blessing the Spirit-State and that the clever manipulating of Soul-journeying is soullessly ruining it?

Experience that the profound Virtuosity of Spirit, our inborn Spirit-nature and Human Soul, is so deeply penetrating and far-reaching that it returns all human beings to the original Unity, Identity, Totality and Harmony of Spirit?

TRANSFORMATIVE PASSAGE 66

HINDERING TO ADVANCING

❖

Great rivers are governing
Hundreds of valley streams
By being below them

As Spirit-identifying human beings
In some ways
Being above ego-identified people
We are conversing below them
Supporting and elevating them
In some ways
Being ahead of ego-identified people
We are following behind them
Backing and advancing them

As Spirit-identifying human beings:
In some ways
Being on top of ego-identified people
We are not burdening them
In some ways
Being in front of ego-identified people
We are not hindering them

Being so, our whole world
Is gladly supporting and backing us
As Spirit-identifying human beings
We are not contending
And there is no contending

EXPLICATIVE SUMMARY ❖ 66

This passage is from our Human Soul's ego-hindering to its Spiritual advancing. Great rivers are governing valley streams and Spirit-identifying human beings are regulating ego-identified people by being below them. Spirit-identifying human beings are supporting and elevating and backing and advancing the Soul-journeying, Soul-working and Soul-making of ego-identified people by being below them and following behind them and by not burdening or hindering them from above or ahead. As such, they themselves are being gladly supported and backed by fellow human beings without contending.

MEDITATIVE INQUIRY ❖ 66

As journeying Souls, can we:

Soulfully relate to fellow human beings from below, supporting and elevating them, and follow them from behind, backing and advancing them; in their Soul-working, Soul-making and Soul-journeying?

As, perhaps in some ways and at some times more Spiritually developed than ego-identified people in our Soul-working, Soul-making and Soul-journeying; not burden and oppress them from above or obstruct and hinder them from ahead and allow them to support and back our own Soul-journeying without contending?

TRANSFORMATIVE PASSAGE 67

FATALITY TO LOVING

❖

Our whole world is saying
Great Spirit is seeming like nothing at all
It is just because of this
That it is being so great
That which is seemng like something
Is not so great

We are having three Spiritual treasures
Deeply cherished and fully embodied
First is unconditioned love[11]
Second is conserved resources
Third is restrained precedence
Unconditioning love, we can be courageous
Conserving resources, we can be generous
Restraining precedence, we can be splendrous

Being courageous without unconditioned love
Being generous without conserved resources
Being splendrous without restrained precedence
Can bring about ruin and death

Through unconditioned loving, we are:
Succeeding in the offensive
Sustaining in the defensive

Heaven's Spirit is protecting and saving us
Through unconditioned loving

EXPLICATIVE SUMMARY ❖ 67

This passage is from our Human Soul's ego-fatality to its Spirit-loving. Some of the greatness of Spirit is related to its Mysterious nonmateriality, invisiblity and ineffability, its being no-'thing' at all. Things that are seeming like some-'thing' are not so great. Some of the greatness of our Human Soul is related to its three Spiritual treasures of uncondition*ed* love, conserved resources and restrained precedence. Spirit-identifying human beings are deeply cherishing and fully embodying the three treasures of our inborn Spirit-nature and Human Soul, i.e., uncondition*ed* love, conserved resources and restrained precedence; by which they can be courageous, generous and splendrous without risking ruin and possibly death. They are sustaining in the defensive and succeeding in the offensive through the protection and salvation of the unconditioned loving of Heaven's Spirit.

MEDITATIVE INQUIRY ❖ 67

As journeying Souls, can we:

Deeply cherish and fully embody our three Spiritual treasures of unconditioned loving, conserved resources and restrained precedence and be courageous, generous and splendrous Human Souls?

Avoid the ruining and demise of our Soul-working, Soul-making, Soul-journeying and possibly our very Human Soul itself by not being courageous without unconditioned love, not being generous without conserved resources and not being splendrous without restrained precedence?

Experience that, through unconditioned loving, we are succeeding in the offensive and sustaining in the defensive during our Soul-working, Soul-making and Soul-journeying and that Spirit is protecting and saving us throughout their duration through unconditioned loving?

CONTENDING TO ULTIMACY

❖

As most Spiritually developed warriors
We are not being hurtful
As most Spiritually developed fighters
We are not being rageful
As most Spiritually developed victors
We are not being vengeful
As most Spiritually developed leaders
We are not being domineering

This is:
The Soulfulness of not contending
The powerfulness of not coercing
Matching the Ultimacy of Heaven's Spirit

EXPLICATIVE SUMMARY ❖ 68

This passage is from our Human Soul's ego-contending to its Spiritual Ultimacy. The potency and efficacy of the Virtuosity of Spirit, our inborn Spirit-nature and Human Soul, inhere in not coercing and not contending with fellow human beings and match the Ultimacy of Heaven's Spirit. Spirit-identifying human beings are Spiritually developed human beings who are not soullessly being domineering, hurtful, rageful and vengeful; even when being leaders, warriors, fighters and victors. Such is the Soulfulness of their non-contending and the powerfulness of their non-coercing that are matching the Ultimacy of Heaven's Spirit.

MEDITATIVE INQUIRY ❖ 68

As journeying Souls, can we:

Not be soullessly domineering, hurtful, rageful and vengeful if and when engaging in unfortunate conflicted relationships with fellow human beings during Soul-working and Soul-making along the way of enSouling and Soul-journeying?

Match the Ultimacy of Heaven's Spirit by not soullessly coercing and contending with fellow human beings during Soul-working and Soul-making along the way of enSouling and Soul-journeying?

TRANSFORMATIVE PASSAGE 69

ENEMIES TO LOVING

❖

As Soulful military strategists:
We are not taking the offensive
And are taking the defensive
We are not advancing an inch
And are retreating a foot

This is:
Deploying forces without marching them
Facing opponents without engaging them
Showing weapons without employing them
Defeating armies without battling them

For us Spirit-identifying human beings
There is no greater disaster
Than creating and attacking enemies
Fighting an enemy is losing
Our Spirit's three treasures

So, when opposing forces are warring
Only uncondition*ed* loving is winning

EXPLICATIVE SUMMARY ❖ 69

This passage is from our Human Soul's ego-enemies to its Spirit-loving. Creating and fighting 'enemies' are losing our Spirit's three treasures and, in any fighting and warring, unconditio*ned* loving is the only 'winner'. Spirit-identifying human beings are Soulfully taking the defensive and not the offensive position in conflicts and are retreating rather than advancing. In any conflicts during their Soul-working, Soul-making and Soul-journeying; they are 'winning' by not soullessly creating, engaging, attacking, battling and defeating opponents and enemies and through preserving their three treasures of Spirit and the courage, generosity and splendor of their unconditio*ned* love, conserved resources and restrained precedence.

MEDITATIVE INQUIRY ❖ 69

As journeying Souls, can we:
Soulfully take the defensive and retreat rather than soullessly take the offensive and advance in conflicted relationships?

Soulfully relate to any opponents by influencing without making aggressive moves, confronting without making direct engagements, displaying without employing powerful instruments and defeating without undergoing actual battling?

Experience that there is no greater human disaster in Soul-working, Soul-making and Soul-journeying than soullessly creating, attacking and fighting 'enemies'; losing Spirit's three treasures of unconditio*ned* loving, conserved resources and restrained precedence while still being courageous, generous and splendrous and, thus, risking ruin and death?

Experience that the only real survivor of; and ultimate 'winner' in; conflicts, fights and wars is the infinite and eternal Spirit and Soul of unconditio*ned* loving that is beyond both peace and warring, victory and defeat, winning and losing and living and dying and that everywhere and always remains after both awakened human beings and dead body counts?

TRANSFORMATIVE PASSAGE 70

NOT UNDERSTANDING TO EMPOWERING

❖

Understanding my words is very easy
Practicing my works is very easy
Yet, few people in our world
Are understanding and practicing them

My words are having an Ancestral Spirit
My works are having a Masterful Soul
Most ego-identified people
Are not understanding this
So, they are not understanding me

The few Spirit-identifying human beings
Who are understanding me
The more are they being empowered

As Spirit-identifying human beings, we are:
Wearing coarse clothes on the outer surface
Bearing precious jewels in our inner depths

EXPLICATIVE SUMMARY ❖ 70

This passage is from our Human Soul's not understanding to its Spiritual empowering. The words and works of Soul-journeying have an empowering Ancestral Spirit and Masterful Soul. Spirit-identifying human beings are understanding the empowering words of Ancestral Spirit and are practicing the empowering works of Masterful Soul in their human lives. They are appearing quite ordinary, common and coarse on their outer surface and are quite extra-ordinary, rare and refined in their inner depths.

MEDITATIVE INQUIRY ❖ 70

As journeying Souls, can we:

Understand the Ancestral Spirit of Spiritual teachings and practice the Masterful Soul of Soulful meditations?

Experience the deep inner vitality, potency and efficacy that accompany opening to and identifying with/*as* the Reality and Virtuosity of Spirit, our inborn Spirit-nature and Human Soul?

Safeguard the precious radiant jewels of our Human Soul deep within our Heart-of-Hearts beneath the outer camouflage of ordinariness, commonness and plainness?

Transformative Passage 71

Sickness to Wellness

❖

Understanding and not acting knowing
Is wellness
Not understanding and acting knowing
Is sickness

Being sick of this sickness
Is not being sick

As Spirit-identifying human beings:
We are being sick of this sickness
By being sick of this sickness
We are not being sick

EXPLICATIVE SUMMARY ❖ 71

This passage is from our Human Soul's ego-sickness to its Spirit-wellness. Understanding Spirit and our Human Soul and not acting knowing is wellness. Not understanding Spirit and our Human Soul and acting knowing is sickness. Spirit-identifying human beings are sick of the sickness of not understanding and acting as if they are knowing the Mysterious, Miraculous, Marvelous and Magnificent workings of Spirit and Soul and are free of this kind of illness.

MEDITATIVE INQUIRY ❖ 71

As journeying Souls, can we:
Be sick of the sickness of thinking, pretending and acting as if we know and understand Spirit and its Mysterious presence, Miraculous workings, Marvelous manifestations and Magnifient completions in/*as* our Human Soul and, therefore, end the sickness?

If fortunate enough to experience the Mysterious, Miraculous, Marvelous and Magnificent Reality of Spirit present, working, manifesting and completing in/*as* our Human Soul; not act as if we understand it like a conceptual objectification of rational thinking, logical reasoning and intellectualized knowledge?

TRANSFORMATIVE PASSAGE 72

DISRESPECT TO AWESOMENESS

❖

As ego-identified people:
When we are not respecting the awesome
The awful is descending upon us

As Spirit-identifying human beings
We are not compressing people's homes
We are not oppressing people's lives
By not doing so
People are not being suppressed
Repressed or depressed

As Spirit-identifying human beings, we are:
Knowing but not displaying ourselves
Valuing but not glorifying ourselves

Rejecting the outer *'that'*/ego
Accepting the inner *'This'*/Spirit

EXPLICATIVE SUMMARY ❖ 72

This passage is from our Human Soul's ego-disrespecting to its Spirit's awesomeness. When ego-identified people are not respecting the awesome, the awful is descending upon them. Spirit-identifying human beings are respecting the awesomeness of Spirit and are Soulfully relating to fellow human beings without soullessly oppressing, suppressing, depressing or impressing them. They are knowing and valuing, but not displaying or glorifying, themselves and are accepting the Reality and ubiquity of Spirit deep within themselves.

MEDITATIVE INQUIRY ❖ 72

As journeying Souls, can we:

Respect the awesome Mysterious Reality and workings of Spirit and avoid having to suffer awful wake-up calls during the dark nights of our Soul-working, Soul-making and Soul-journeying?

Not compress the free Spirit and not oppress the deep Soul of fellow human beings with prescriptive dogmatic teachings and constrictive ritualistic practices?

Understand, accept, experience and value our inborn Spirit-nature, our Human Soul, as just and all 'This' and not glorify or display it as an object in the outer social world of fellow human beings?

KUEI

歸

RETURN/REVERT
GO OR COME BACK
TO WHERE ONE BELONGS

HSIANG

鄉

ONE'S NATIVE PLACE
THE COUNTRY
VILLAGE/HAMLET

THE COMPLETING OF OUR HUMAN SOUL'S WAYFARING JOURNEYING AND THAT OF OUR SPIRITUAL FRIENDS AND COMPANIONS IS A ROUND-TRIP RETURNING BACK TO THE PLACE OF ORIGIN. THIS RETURNING IS A COMING HOME TO TAO/SPIRIT, THE CULMINATING DWELLING PLACE OF SOJOURNING PILGRIMS, WHERE WE NATURALLY BELONG AND FROM WHICH WE NEVER EVER REALLY LEFT.

TRANSFORMATIVE PASSAGE 73

DARING TO COMPLETING

❖

Being courageous by daring is risking dying
Being courageous by not daring is valuing living
Of these two, at times
One is being helpful
One is being harmful
Who is knowing why Heaven's Spirit
Is preferring what it does?
Even Spirit-identifying human beings
Are not always being certain

Heaven's Spirit is:
Sustaining without striving
Responding without speaking
Attracting without inviting
Completing without planning

The network of Heaven's Spirit
Is vast and wide-meshed
Yet nothing and no one
Are slipping through

EXPLICATIVE SUMMARY ❖ 73

This passage is from our Human Soul's ego-daring to its Spirit-completing. Heaven's Spirit is attracting, responding, sustaining and completing in our Soul-journeying and its vast and wide-meshed network lets no Human Soul slip through. Spirit-identifying human beings are valuing living and are courageously not daring and risking dying. Like Heaven's Spirit, they are attracting without inviting, responding without speaking, sustaining without striving, completing without planning and interconnecting without neglecting.

MEDITATIVE INQUIRY ❖ 73

As journeying Souls, can we:

Be courageous without daring, soullessly devaluing living, risking dying and not completing our Soul-working, Soul-making and Soul-journeying?

Accept not always knowing what is helpful and/or harmful for our Soul-working, Soul-making and Soul-journeying in the Mysterious workings of Spirit?

Identify with/*as* Spirit and its working in our Soul-making and be attracting, responding, sustaining and completing in our Soul-working without inviting, speaking, striving or planning?

Be reassured that, even after the longest ego-falls, we finally land in the safety net of Spirit?

TRANSFORMATIVE PASSAGE 74

KILLING TO SACREDNESS

❖

As ego-identified people
If we are not fearing dying
Why be threatening us
With death penalties?

As ego-identified people
Even if we are fearing dying
And murderers are being captured
Who is daring to execute them?

Only Great Executioner Spirit
Is killing the killers
Substituting for Great Executioner Spirit
Is like replacing a master carpenter
Taking over for a master carpenter
We are usually injuring our own hands

EXPLICATIVE SUMMARY ❖ 74

This passage is from our Human Soul's ego-killing to its Spiritual Sacredness. Only Spirit, as Great Executioner, is in charge of executing the destiny and fate of the living and dying of our Human Souls. Spirit-identifying human beings are trusting and respecting that the presence, agency and workings of Spirit in our human world are implementing and executing the living and dying of fellow human beings and are not attempting to be a substitute or replacement for Spirit by taking such matters as killing Sacred human life into their own hands and risking injuring their Human Soul.

MEDITATIVE INQUIRY ❖ 74

As journeying Souls, can we:

Value living, not fear dying, honor the Sacredness and preciousness of Spirit, Soul and Life and not soullessly kill fellow human beings even if they themselves are killers of fellow human beings?

Refrain from attempting to substitute for or to replace Spirit and its agency in the human world and refrain from taking the fate of fellow human beings into our own hands and risking injuring our Human Soul and harming our Soul-making work?

Trust in the Mysterious workings of Spirit to dispense punishment and exact retribution to those soulless people who violate the sanctity and terminate the viability of human life and who abuse the integrity and desecrate the dignity of the Human Soul?

TRANSFORMATIVE PASSAGE 75

STRIVING TO TREASURING

❖

As ego-identified people
We are going hungry
Because as ego-identified leaders
We are taxing too much
So, we are starving

As ego-identifed people
We are acting unruly
Because as ego-identified leaders
We are ruling too much
So, we are rebelling

As ego-identified people
We are ignoring mortality
Because as ego-identified leaders
We are demanding too much
So, we are toiling

As Spirit-identifying human beings
Rather than busily striving for a life
We are Soulfully treasuring living

EXPLICATIVE SUMMARY ❖ 75

This passage is from our Human Soul's ego-striving to its Spiritual treasuring. Human beings; when only collectively regarded as 'the people', 'them', anonymous ciphers in the general public and mass humanity; can be soullessly subjected to the forceful controls and fanciful whims of ego-identified domineering authority figures in leadership positions and, as a result, suffer being infantalized, patronized, marginalized, dehumanized and victimized by their abuses of power and, so, become impoverished, rebellious and despirited. Spirit-identifying human beings, when in leadership positions, are not soullessly overtaxing, overruling and overdemanding of fellow human beings who, as a result, are not being impoverished, rebellious and overworked. Spirit-identifying human beings are Soulfully treasuring the sheer and utter and pure and simple reality of living life and are not busily and stressfully striving to 'make' a living.

MEDITATIVE INQUIRY ❖ 75

As journeying Souls, can we:

When in leadership positions and roles; not be soullessly taxing, controlling and demanding but, rather, be Soulfully fair, supporting and inspiring and treat fellow human beings equally and impartially as fellow journeying Souls?

Soulfully not strive for life or force fellow human beings to fight and struggle for life but, rather, plainly and simply treasure the living Reality of Spirit, the vital energy of our Human Soul and the sheer and utter experience of being alive as an embodied Spirit/body-Spirit and an inSpirited body/Spirit-body?

Soulfully live and intimately share the Mystery of originating, the Miracles of forming, the Marvels of manifestating and the Magnificence of completing of Soul-working, Soul-making and Soul-journeying; the enSouling of our Human Self, Human Being and being human?

TRANSFORMATIVE PASSAGE 76

RIGIDITY TO FLUIDITY

❖

At birth, we are being soft and fluid
At death, we are being hard and rigid
Grasses, trees and all living beings
When alive, are being tender and flexible
When dead, are being withered and brittle

Hard and rigid
Are accompanying dying
Soft and fluid
Are accompanying living

So,
Fixed armies will be shattered
Stiff branches will be snapped

Being hard and rigid
Is soullessly least developed
Being soft and fluid
Is Soulfully most developed

EXPLICATIVE SUMMARY ❖ 76

This passage is from our Human Soul's ego-rigidity to its Spiritual flexibility and fluidity. Living Soulful beings are soft, flexible and fluid and dead soulless beings are hard, brittle and rigid. Spirit-identifying human beings are soft, tender, flexible and flowing in the ongoing conducting of Soul-work, Soul-making and Soul-journeying and in the lifelong cultivating of Spirit. They are human beings who are embodying, living and enacting the energetic viability, vitality and vibrancy of our developed Human Soul's aliveness.

MEDITATIVE INQUIRY ❖ 76

As journeying Souls, can we:
Be and live the vital Reality and life energies of Spirit and our Human Soul, the softness and tenderness of an embodied Spirit and the flexibility and fluidity of an inSpirited body and not have Spirit and our Human Soul become hard, rigid, withered, brittle and easily broken?

TRANSFORMATIVE PASSAGE 77

PEOPLE'S WAY TO SPIRIT'S WAY

❖

Heaven's Spirit is like drawing a bow
What is higher is being lowered
What is lower is being elevated
What is longer is being shortened
What is shorter is being extended

Heaven's Spirit is:
Reducing the excessive
Supplementing the insufficient
People's ego is:
Diminishing the deficient
Augmenting the superfluous

Who is having sufficient abundance
To be offering our world?
Only Spirit-identifying human beings
Embodying Spirit

As Spirit-identifying human beings, we are:
Benefiting all without needing gratitude
Completing works without claiming credit
Not desiring to be displayng excellence

EXPLICATIVE SUMMARY ❖ 77

This passage is from our Human Soul's ego-ways to its Spirit-Way. The workings of Spirit are naturally compensating, counterbalancing and equalizing. Spirit-identifying human beings are embodying and enacting Spirit; are reducing the excessive and supplementing the insufficient and are having sufficient abundance to be benefiting fellow human beings and to be completing Soul-working, Soul-making and Soul-journeying without displaying excellence, claiming credit or needing gratitude.

MEDITATIVE INQUIRY ❖ 77

As journeying Souls, can we:

Identify with/*as*, embody and enact the workings of Spirit rather than those of ego-identified people and Soulfully reduce the excessive and supplement the insufficient rather than soullessly diminish the already deficient and augment the already superfluous in Soul-working and Soul-making?

Embody, offer and share the abundantly sufficient vital energies of Spirit and its Virtuosity, our inborn Spirit-nature and Human Soul, with fellow human beings in our world?

Conduct and be completing our Soul-working, Soul-making and Soul-journeying and benefit the Soul-working, Soul-making and Soul-journeying of fellow human beings without displaying excellence, claiming credit or needing gratitude?

TRANSFORMATIVE PASSAGE 78

ROUGHNESS TO GENTLENESS

❖

Nothing in our world
Is being softer and gentler than water
Yet, nothing is surpassing it
For overcoming hard and rough
Nothing is replacing it

Our whole world is knowing
Gentleness is overcoming roughness
Softness is overcoming hardness
Yet, few of us are practicing it

As Spirit-identifying human beings
We are saying:
Bearing the inner shame of our ego-state
Is being Spiritual custodian of the land
Enduring the outer misery of our ego-state
Is being Soulful steward of the world

True words are seeming paradoxical

EXPLICATIVE SUMMARY ❖ 78

This passage is from our Human Soul's ego-hardness and rough-ness to its Spirit-softness and gentleness. Nothing in our world is more soft and gentle than water, yet nothing equals its unsurpassable and irreplacable power and abilty to overcome hardness and roughness. Spirit-identifying human beings are softly and gently empathizing and identifying with the inner shame and outer misery of our human con-dition and, as such, are being Spiritual custodians and Soulful stew-ards of our human world and our fellow human beings.

MEDITATIVE INQUIRY ❖ 78

As journeying Souls, can we:

Overcome the hard times and rough spots of our Soul-working, Soul-making and Soul-journeying by being the water-like softness and gentleness of the vital energy and efficacious Virtuosity of Spirit, our inborn Spirit-nature and Human Soul?

Experience, empathize and identify with the inner shame and outer misery of our human condition and the ego-states of fellow human beings and be Spiritual and Soulful custodians, guardians and stewards of a Spiritual and Soulful world of real and true Human Beings?

TRANSFORMATIVE PASSAGE 79

BLAMING TO RESPONSIBILTY

❖

As great grievances are being reconciled
Some discontent is usually remaining
How is this being made good?

As Spirit-identifying human beings:
We are owning our part in the matters
Without blaming the other parties

Being with Soul and Soulful
We are responsibly fulfilling agreements
Being without Soul and soulless
We are vindictively demanding reciprocations

Heaven's Spirit is being impartial
It is constantly serving goodness

EXPLICATIVE SUMMARY ❖ 79

This passage is from our Human Soul's ego-blaming to its Spiritual responsibility. When great disagreements and conflicts are sufficiently reconciled and resolved, some unsettledness and discontent may still be remaining which can be improved by Soulfully taking full responsibility for our part in the matters. Spirit-identifying human beings are Soulfully and responsibly owning and fully acknowledging their part in disagreements and conflicts and are not soullessly blaming or vindictively demanding reciprocation from fellow human beings. In such matters, they are embodying, personifying and enacting the goodness and impartiality of Heaven's Spirit.

MEDITATIVE INQUIRY ❖ 79

As journeying Souls, can we:
Successfully complete disagreements or conflicts by Soulfully taking full responsibility for our part in them and not soullessly blaming fellow human beings who are party to them?

In keeping with the Virtuosity of Spirit, our inborn Spirit-nature and Human Soul, responsibly and Soulfully fulfill agreements with fellow human beings and not vindictively and soullessly demand reciprocations from them?

Identify with/*as*, embody, personify and enact the inherent goodness, fairness and kindness of Spirit, our inborn Spirit-nature and Human Soul, in impartially relating to fellow human beings throughout our Soul-working, Soul-making and Soul-journeying?

TRANSFORMATIVE PASSAGE 80

CIVILIZATION TO CONTENTMENT

❖

Here is a small Spirit-State
With few inhabitants

As Spirit-identifying human beings:
Though there are one hundred times
The necessary conveniences
We are not using them
We are taking dying seriously
And are not traveling far away
Though there are enough vehicles
We are not riding in them
Though there are some weapons
We are not needing them

As Spirit-identifying human beings, we are:
Living simply and sufficiently
Being satisfied with our local foods
Being pleased with our plain clothes
Being contented with our cozy homes
Being delighted with our usual lives

Neighboring communities are within earshot
Of crowing roosters and barking dogs
Yet, as Spirit-identifying human beings
We are happily growing old and dying
Without going to visit them

EXPLICATIVE SUMMARY ❖ 80

This passage is from our Human Soul's civilization to its Spiritual contentment. The vast domain of Spirit can essentially, physically and existentially manifest itself as a small intimate State and State of Being populated and inhabited by only a few indwelling Soulful human beings who are enjoying living simply and simply living. Spirit-identifying human beings are not needing or using conveniences, vehicles and weapons; are satisfied, pleased contented and delighted with their local foods, plain clothes, cozy homes and usual lives; are taking living and dying seriously; are not traveling far away or visiting neighboring communities and are happily being together and contentedly growing old with each other.

MEDITATIVE INQUIRY ❖ 80

As journeying Souls, can we:
    Take living and dying seriously, not travel far from home, not soullessly waste our precious lifetime and squander our valuable energies and not become soullessly lost in the convenient complexities of so-called civilization, e.g., gadgets of mass production, desires of mass proportion, goods of mass consumption, vehicles of mass transportation, entertainments of mass distraction, institutions of mass corruption, weapons of mass destruction, etc., and, instead, live a more natural and less complicated life of Spirit and Human Soul?
    Be living smaller and more simply, sufficiently and Soulfully; satisfied, pleased, contented and delighted with our local foods, plain clothes, cozy dwellings and usual lives?
    Enjoy remaining and residing in our small community, living intimately and peacefully with our fellow Soul-journeying Spiritual companions, growing old happily and contentedly and dying fulfilled without necessarily traveling to other places or needing to visit human beings in nearby surrounding communities?

CONTENDING TO ASSISTING

❖

Soulful words are not always beautiful
Beautiful words are not always Soulful

Soulful human beings are not always arguing
Arguing people are not always Soulful

Soulful human beings are not always learned
Learned people are not always Soulful

As Spirit-identifying human beings:
We are not accumulating
The more we are giving to others
The more we are receiving
The more we are using for others
The more we are obtaining

Heaven's Spirit
Is benefiting, not harming
Human Being's Soul
Is assisting, not contending

EXPLICATIVE SUMMARY ❖ 81

This passage is from our Human Soul's ego-contending to its Spiritual benefiting and Soulful assisting. The real Way and workings of Spirit and the true Pathways and passages of Soul are to benefit and assist and to not harm and contend with human beings as fellow Soul-journeyers. Spirit-identifying and Soulful human beings are not always erudite, articulate and disputatious. They are contributing who they are and donating what they have to fellow human beings and are being of Spiritual benefit and Soulful assistance to them without harming or contending.

MEDITATIVE INQUIRY ❖ 81

As journeying Souls, can we:
   Soulfully speak words even when they may not be beautiful and not soullessly use Spiritual rhetoric and jargon to display erudition or to argue with fellow human beings?
   Not soullessly collect and accumulate things, goods, money, people, Spiritual merit, etc. and experience that our real wealth and true abundance are measured by what we naturally receive and obtain from how much we donate and contribute to the Soul-working and Soul-making of fellow Human Beings as Soul-journeying companions and kindred Spirits?
   Identify with/*as* Spirit, Spiritually benefit and not harm, and Soulfully assist and not contend with, fellow Human Beings as Soul-journeying companions and kindred Spirits?[12]

I

一

ALL/THE WHOLE OF
PRIMORDIAL UNITY
THE FIRST/SOURCE
SAME/ALIKE/UNIFORM

TZ'U

此

THIS
HERE
NOW
LIKE THIS

JU

如

AS
LIKE
SAME AS
EQUAL TO

CHE

這

THIS
HERE
NOW
RIGHT NOW

AFTER RUNNING, STOPPING, TURNING AROUND AND CONVERSING;
WE ARE ARRIVING AT TAO/SPIRIT, OUR INNERMOST, DEEPEST,
CENTERMOST, TRUEST AND UTMOST SPIRITUAL AND SOULFUL NATURE
WHICH IS ALL THIS/AS THIS/HERE AND NOW! TAO, OUR ONE SPIRIT
AND TE, OUR UNIQUE HUMAN SOUL, ARE ALL THAT IS/AS IT IS,
ALL AROUND US, ALL WITHIN US, ALL BETWEEN US AND
ALL BEYOND US.

APPENDIX ONE
TWIN SOULS

The following listings; which are not exclusive, comprehensive, exhaustive nor definitive; identify some of the realities; qualities, characteristics and attributes; relationships; activities, functions and operations and personifications integrating our twin physical/body Soul and Spiritual/Spirit Soul between which reciprocal passages are constantly being made.

Physical/Body Soul/P'o	Spiritual/Spirit Soul/Hun
Realities	
acquired/cultivated Ch'i energy	bestowed/primordial Ch'i energy
Ch'i energy descending/condensing	Ch'i energy ascending/radiating
embodied Spirit/body-Spirit	inSpirited body/Spirit-body
incarnate/incorporated	disincarnate/animated
Miracles/Marvels	Mystery/Magnificence
ego/mind/body	Self/Psyche/Spirit
things/others/world	Beings/Souls/Cosmos
actuality/Virtuosity	Reality/Virtuality
intelligence/wisdom	Reason/Truth
process/pattern/rules	Principle/Design/Law
relative/multiple/diverse	Absolute/One/Identity
being/presence/fullness	Nonbeing/No-thingness/Void
Earthly/terrestrial	Heavenly/celestial
Qualities/Characteristics/Attributes	
finite/temporal/mortal	infinite/eternal/immortal
natural/creature-like	supernatural/divine-like
created/born/derived	uncreated/unborn/original
differentiated/compounded	undifferentiated/pure
material/physical/formed	nonmateial/nonphysical/formless
existential/phenomenal	essential/transphenomenal
immanent/personal/intimate	transcendent/transpersonal/ultimate
actual/manifest/apparent	potential/latent/hidden
explicit/disclosed/revealed	implicit/concealed/secret
concrete/solid/describable	abstract/ephemeral/ineffable
situated/dimensional	ubiquitous/nondimensional
bounded/limited/closed	boundless/limitless/open
dependent/conditioned	independent/unconditioned

individual/unique	universal/general
differential/partial/incomplete	integral/whole/complete
divided/dual/polar	undivided/nondual/transpolar
changing/variable	constant/regular
impermanent/temporary/transient	permanent/enduring/perpetual
gross/dense/coarse	subtle/delicate/refined
below/behind/within/between	above/ahead/around/beyond
centripetal/contracting	centrigual/expanding
condensing/congealing/coalescing	radiating/dispersing/evanescing
aims/goals/objectives	teleological/destined/eschatological
projects/purposes/plans	spontaneous/purposeless/unplanned
earth-/water-/valley-like	air-/fire-/mountain-like

Activities/Functions/Operations

realizing/actualizing	creating/generating
incarnating/internalizing	originating/sourcing
assimilating/identifying	pervading/encompassing
conserving/cultivating Ch'i energy	animating/vitalizing Ch'i energy
nourishing/supporting	activating/energizing
serving/assisting/benefiting	blessing/protecting/sustaining
individuating/personifying	potentiating/developing
manifesting/enacting	regulating/guiding
receiving/reflecting	transforming/harmonizing
responding/returning	evolving/culminating

Personifications

Te Jen/Te-like/Soul-like	Tao Jen/Tao-like/Spirit-like
Soulful/radiant/charismatic	Spiritual/luminous/numinous
true/genuine/wise	real/pure/enlightened
actualized/liberated	realized/free
grounded/centered	centered/spacious
integrated/balanced	unified/identified
aware/open/accepting/calm	awake/clear/empty/still
equality/empathic	impartiality/compassionate
talented/capable/skillful	gifted/endowed/genius
humble/modest/excellent	great/supreme/splendid
ordinary/simple	extraordinary/vast
fulfilled/concluded/completed	culminated/perfected/whole
developed/evolved	Sacred/Holy

APPENDIX TWO
PERSONAL SOUL

The following listings identify our Personal Soul or Self Soul as the mediating integration of the bipolar nature of our twin Spiritual/Spirit Soul and our physical/body Soul. Our personal/Self Soul can be experienced as the still centerpoint and/or pivotal axis of some of our Human Soul's reciprocal passages between Spirit and body in the Heart center of our human body. This paradigm can also be used as a model for the intermediating and integrating linking of any other transformative passages in our Soul-work, Soul-making and Soul-journeying.

Spiritual/Spirit Soul	Personal/Self Soul	Physical/Body Soul
All That Is	This	As It Is
Everywhere At Once	Is	Here and Now
Heavenly nature	Human nature	Earthly nature
Yang Ch'i energies	Yin/Yang Ch'i energies	Yin Ch'i energies
Divine Being	Human being	Creature being
Spirit	Spirit-body/body-Spirit	body
Psyche	Heart-Mind	mind
Self	oneself	ego
divinity	humanity	creaturehood
Spirituality	personality	physicality
transpersonal	interpersonal	nonpersonal
supraconscious	conscious	unconscious
all one/everyone	this one/someone	no one/anyone
universality	individuality	collectivity
identity	equality	diversity
totality	unity	multiplicity
boundless	boundaried	bounded
open/expanded	pulsating	closed/contracted
subjects	subject-objects	things
Beings	selves	others
Cosmos	culture	world
Reality	actuality	nonreality
Truth	wisdom	illusion
Principle	process	content
Design	plan	impulse

Spiritual/Spirit Soul	Personal/Self Soul	Physical/Body Soul
Law	self-regulation	rules
Mystery/Magnificence	Miracles/Marvels	occurrences/events
Reason	intelligence	nonrationality
illumination	insight/intuition	instinct
awake	aware	asleep
vision	imagination	dream/fantasy
transcendence	acculturation	trance
meaning/purpose	interrelation	structure/function
independent	interdependent	dependent
unconditioned	choiceful	conditioned
liberated	committed	determined
reflexive/recursive	receptive/responsive	resistive/reactive
non-attached	interconnected	attached
trusting	experimenting	controlling
according/agreeing	attuning/accomodating	aligning/adjusting
contemplative	cooperative/collaborative	competetive
peace/harmony	negotiation	conflict/contention
simplicity	reduction	complexity
sufficiency	adequacy	insufficiency
security	contentment	insecurity
meditation	mediation	medication
Spiritual strength	personal empowerment	physical force
completion/culmination	consummation/fulfillment	concluding/ending
ecstasty/bliss	happiness/joy/delight	unhappiness

APPENDIX THREE
CARTOGRAPHIES

The passaging journeying of our ubiquitous Human Soul throughout its interweaving life-coursing, life-cycling and life-spanning; from our being ego-identified to being Spirit-identified; is n-dimensional, multi-dimensional, omni-directional and polyphasic and its realities cannot be depicted in any one-dimensional, linear and uni-directional way. However, the following maps of the Human Soul and the enSouling process may be of some heuristic value in showing some developmental vectors, trajectories, directions and trendings of their ascending/descending and progressing/retrogressing within human consciousness and experience, as well as their enSouling/deSouling and integrating and dissociating.

CARTOGRAPHY OF THE HUMAN SOUL – 1
Soul-Identifications

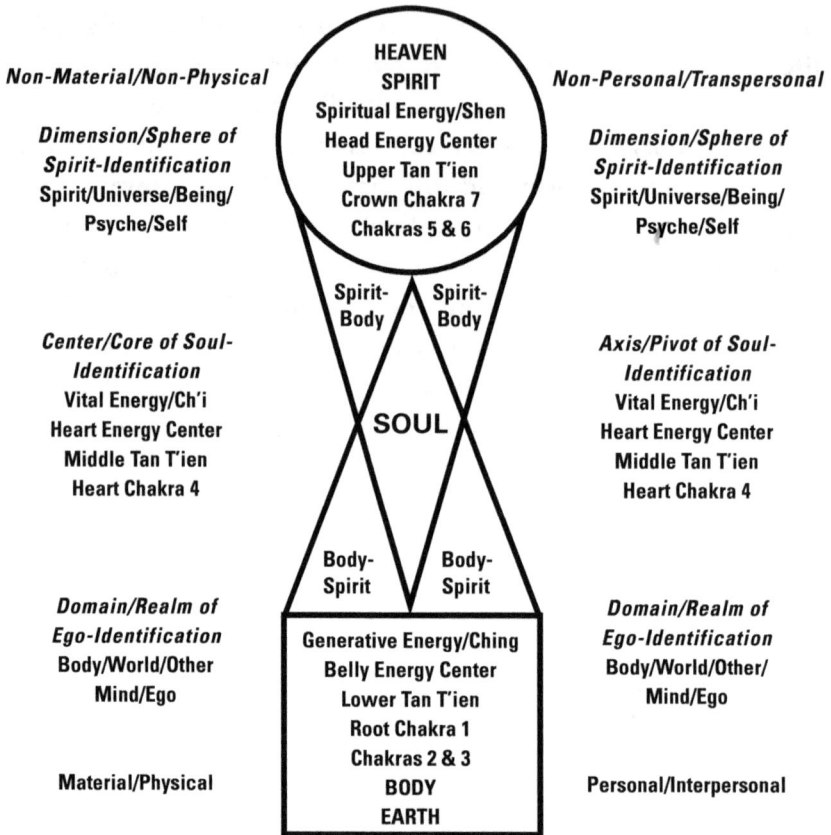

Non-Material/Non-Physical

Dimension/Sphere of
Spirit-Identification
Spirit/Universe/Being/
Psyche/Self

Center/Core of Soul-
Identification
Vital Energy/Ch'i
Heart Energy Center
Middle Tan T'ien
Heart Chakra 4

Domain/Realm of
Ego-Identification
Body/World/Other
Mind/Ego

Material/Physical

Non-Personal/Transpersonal

Dimension/Sphere of
Spirit-Identification
Spirit/Universe/Being/
Psyche/Self

Axis/Pivot of Soul-
Identification
Vital Energy/Ch'i
Heart Energy Center
Middle Tan T'ien
Heart Chakra 4

Domain/Realm of
Ego-Identification
Body/World/Other/
Mind/Ego

Personal/Interpersonal

HEAVEN
SPIRIT
Spiritual Energy/Shen
Head Energy Center
Upper Tan T'ien
Crown Chakra 7
Chakras 5 & 6

Spirit-Body   Spirit-Body

SOUL

Body-Spirit   Body-Spirit

Generative Energy/Ching
Belly Energy Center
Lower Tan T'ien
Root Chakra 1
Chakras 2 & 3
BODY
EARTH

CARTOGRAPHY OF THE HUMAN SOUL – 2
Soul Quadrants and Axes

HEAVEN

Embodied Spirit	↑	Spiritual Dimension
Incorporation of Spirit	Spirit	Spirit-identified
Body-Spirit	Universe	*Spirit-Spirit*
Heaven-Body	Being	Heaven-Spirit
Celestial Body	Psyche	Celestial Spirit
Integral Soul	Self	*Spiritual Soul/Hun*
	↓	

EARTH ←→ Body World Others Mind Ego **SOUL** Self Psyche Being Universe Spirit ←→ **HEAVEN**

Bodily Domain	Ego ↑	InSpirited Body
Ego-Identified	Mind	Animation of Body
Body-Body	Others	*Spirit-Body*
Earth-Body	World	Earth-Spirit
Terrestrial Body	Body	Terrestrial Spirit
Physical Soul/P'o	↓	*Integral Soul*

EARTH

CARTOGRAPHY OF THE HUMAN SOUL – 3
EnSouling and DeSouling

Vertical/Spatial Evolving EnSouling

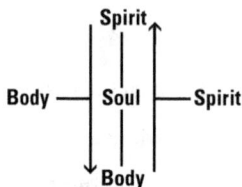

Spirit descending forming a Body-Spirit
Embodied Spirit/Incorporation
Body ascending forming a Spirit-Body
InSpirited body/Animation

Horizontal/Temporal Evolving EnSouling

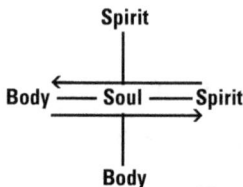

Spirit retrogressing forming a Body-Spirit
Embodied Spirit/Incorporation
Body progressing forming a Spirit-Body
 InSpirited body/Animation

Fractional/Divisional Devolved DeSouling

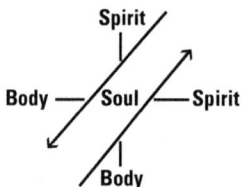

Spirit devolved/regressed to body only
Body evolved/egressed to Spirit only
DeSpirited body and disembodied Spirit
Forming body-body or Spirit-Spirit only
Spasm of dry flesh = horror of the Soul
Schism of thin vapor = terror of the Soul

Integral/Nondual Evolved EnSouling

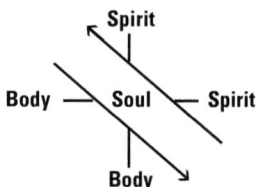

Spirit integrated with body
Body integrated with Spirit
Embodied Spirit and InSpirited body
Forming body-Spirit and Spirit-body
Solid body-Spirit = power of the Soul
Fluid Spirit-body = freedom of the Soul

CARTOGRAPHY OF THE HUMAN SOUL – 4

Soul As Embodying Spirit

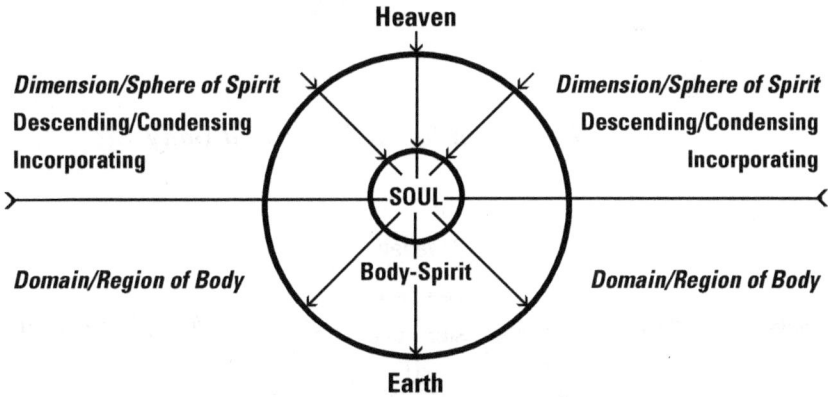

Heaven

Dimension/Sphere of Spirit
Descending/Condensing
Incorporating

Dimension/Sphere of Spirit
Descending/Condensing
Incorporating

SOUL

Domain/Region of Body   **Body-Spirit**   *Domain/Region of Body*

Earth

Soul As InSpiriting Body

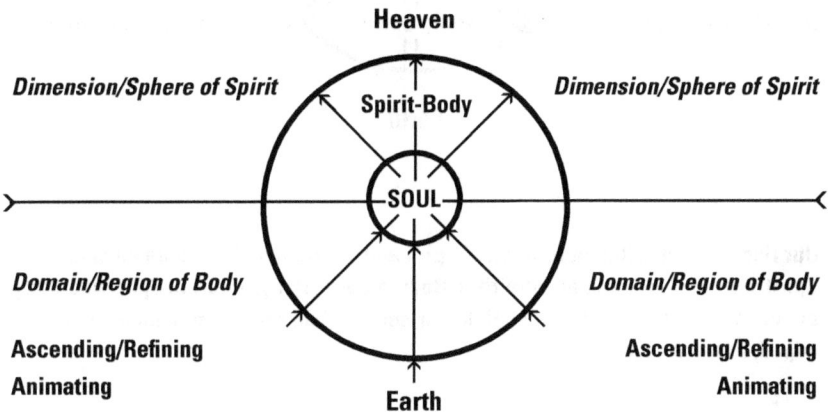

Heaven

Dimension/Sphere of Spirit   **Spirit-Body**   *Dimension/Sphere of Spirit*

SOUL

Domain/Region of Body   *Domain/Region of Body*

Ascending/Refining
Animating

Ascending/Refining
Animating

Earth

Great Heavenly Yang Ch'i Energy descends from the dimension/sphere of Spirit into Earth and condenses in the domain/region of the Human Body, embodying/incorporating as the Physical Nature of our Human Soul or Body-Spirit.

Great Earthly Yin Ch'i Energy ascends from the domain/region of Body into Heaven and refines in the dimension/sphere of Spirit, inSpiriting/animating as the Spiritual Nature of our Human Soul or Spirit-Body.

CARTOGRAPHY OF THE HUMAN SOUL – 5

Soul As Embodied Spirit/InSpirited Body

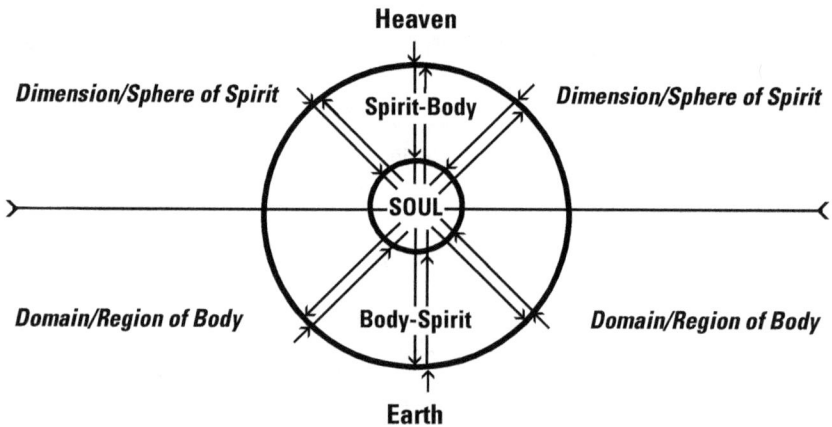

Our Human Soul is the integration of Spirit and our Human Body, both an Embodied Spirit, a Body-Spirit and an InSpirited Body, a Spirit-Body; wherein Spirit and Body are not separated, denied, dissociated or negated but, rather, are united, acknowledged, associated and affirmed.

CARTOGRAPHY OF THE HUMAN SOUL – 6

Disembodied Spirit

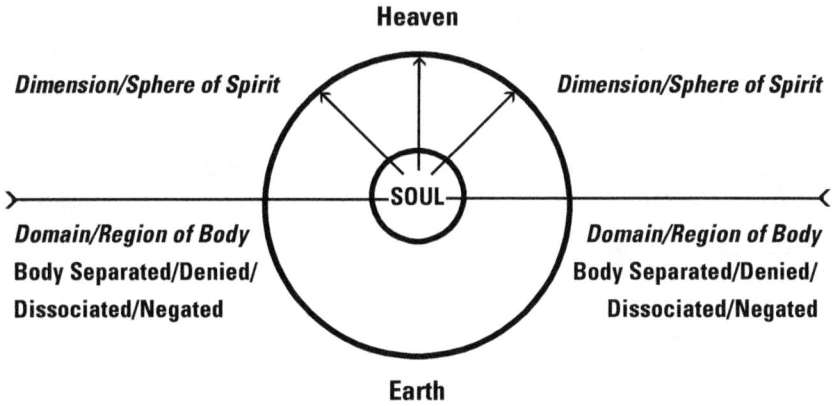

Heaven

Dimension/Sphere of Spirit

Dimension/Sphere of Spirit

SOUL

Domain/Region of Body
Body Separated/Denied/
Dissociated/Negated

Domain/Region of Body
Body Separated/Denied/
Dissociated/Negated

Earth

Despirited Body

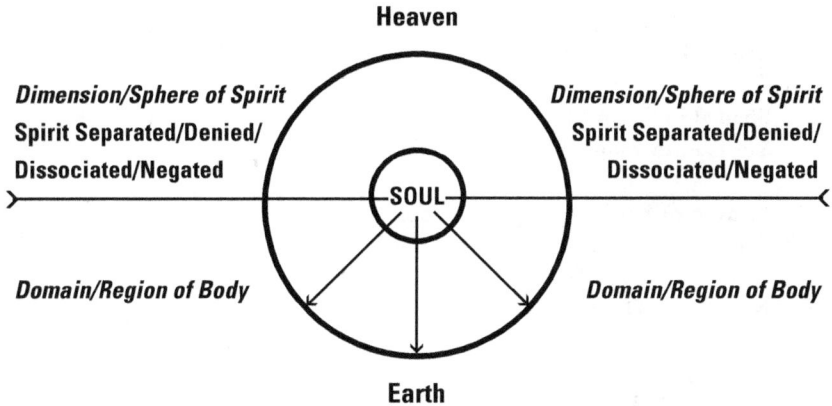

Heaven

Dimension/Sphere of Spirit
Spirit Separated/Denied/
Dissociated/Negated

Dimension/Sphere of Spirit
Spirit Separated/Denied/
Dissociated/Negated

SOUL

Domain/Region of Body

Domain/Region of Body

Earth

Horror is quasi-human existence as a despirited body wherein Spirit is separated, denied, dissociated or negated and only the body is identified with as oneself. Existence is likened to being a dark spasmodic mass of dried meat longing for rain.

Terror is quasi-human existence as a disembodied Spirit wherein body is separated, denied, dissociated or negated and only Spirit is identified with as oneself. Existence is likened to being a dark schismatic chasm of gaseous vapor fearing the wind.

APPENDIX FOUR
ESSENTIAL TRANSFORMATIVE PASSAGES

The following are elaborated references to essential transformative passages of our Human Soul that are contained within the bipolarities of the main experiential concepts and other concepts occurring in the rendition. Included for each of the passages considered are opening excerpts, symbolic images, living processes, relevant descriptions and meditations.

	TRANSFORMATIVE PASSAGE	SYMBOLIC IMAGE	LIVING PROCESS
0	Non- to Supreme Ultimate Wu to T'ai Chi	Mystery Hsuan	Originating Yuan
1	Tao to Virtuosity Tao to Te	Mother Mu	Birthing Sheng
2	Shaded to Sunny Yin Ch'i to Yang Ch'i	Breath Ch'i	Vitalizing Huo
3	Heaven to Earth T'ien to Ti	Soil T'u	Grounding Chi
4	Nothing to Doing Wu to Wei	Water Shui	Nourishing Yang
5	Spirit to Body Shen to Shen	Belly Tu/Fu	Embodying T'i
6	Sacred to Human Being Sheng to Jen	Heart Hsin	Centering Chung
7	Body to Spirit Shen to Ling	Head T'ou	InSpiriting Ku

Transformative Passage 0

TAO/SPIRIT'S NON- TO SUPREME ULTIMATE/WU CHI TO T'AI CHI

Tao/Spirit is birthing One. One is birthing Two. Two is birthing Three. Three is birthing All Beings. (# 42).

The cosmogonic sequencing of Tao/Spirit's originating, forming, manifesting and completing is evolving from the Great Void of Ultimateless Non-Being/No-thingness/Wu Chi to the Great Monad of Primordial Ch'i energy/Yuan Ch'i to the Great Dyad of Yin Ch'i/Yang Ch'i energies to the Great Triad of the Supreme Ultimate/T'ai Chi (Wu Chi + Yin/Yang Ch'i) and, finally, to the Great Myriad of the '10,000 things'/Wan Wu of being/existing in our conscious experiencing.

SYMBOLIC IMAGE ❖ MYSTERY/HSUAN

Mystery and Miracles are one and the same...the gateway of all Wondrous Marvels. (# 1).

The originating of matter is a Mystery, its forming of edges is a Miracle, its manifesting is a Marvel and its developmental completing is a Magnificence. Tao/Spirit's Mystery is concealed within Marvels and Marvels are its revealed Mystery. The awesome Mystery of how something Miraculously arises from the No-Thing of Tao/Spirit is absolutely Marvelous and Wondrous and the Marvels are absolutely Mysterious and Splendid.

LIVING PROCESS ❖ ORIGINATING/YUAN

All beings are originating from Being. Being is originating from Tao/Spirit's Non-Being. (# 40).

Meditate on Tao/Spirit's awesome Mysterious creating of something from its No-'thing'-ness. From where and how does the human heartbeat originate in the cardiac tissue of an in utero human fetus?

Transformative Passage 1

TAO/SPIRIT TO TAO/SPIRIT'S SOUL/TAO TO TE

The intrinsic nature of Great Virtuosity/Te/Soul is uniquely individualizing Tao/Spirit alone. (#21).

Our Human Soul's passaging from Tao/Spirit to its Tao/Spirit-nature/Virtuosity/Te is its uniquely individualizing the intimate actuality of Human Beings as an immanent microcosmic hologram of its transcendent macrocosmic Ultimate Reality. This passaging is from Tao/Spirit to our innermost, deepest, centermost, truest and utmost Tao/Spirit-nature or Human Soul and is the essential Heart of Soul-journeying, Soul-work, Soul-making and the enSouling process occurring throughout our human life course, life cycle and life span.

SYMBOLIC IMAGE ❖ MOTHER/MU

Our world has a beginning which is being called 'Mother'...Embracing Mother is being free from endangering throughout our whole lifetime. (# 52).

Great Mother Tao/Spirit originates Human Life and nourishes and develops it in the Matrix of Her Being and Miraculously brings it forth as Her progeny in the form of a Human Child, through the gateway of its birthing Human Mother. Each newborn Human Child, welcomed and greeted with gratitude and joy, constantly reaffirms the Mystery, Miracles and Marvels of the uniquely individualized Life of Tao/Spirit and the continual hope for, and promise of, the unlimited possibilities of our Human Soul.

LIVING PROCESS ❖ BIRTHING/SHENG

Tao's Valley Spirit is...this Mysterious Feminine, the Root-Source of Heaven-Earth. (# 21).

Meditate on the radiant beauty of birthing mothers' Human Soul as they bring new Human Beings into this Life. Might some of these children transform our world into a more friendly, habitable and sustainable one?[13]

Transformative Passage 2

TAO/SPIRIT'S SHADEDNESS TO SUNNINESS/YIN CH'I TO YANG CH'I

All beings are bearing dark Yin on their backs and harboring bright Yang in their arms. (# 42).

Our Human Soul's passaging from Tao/Spirit's Yin Ch'i energy to its Yang Ch'i energy is the reciprocal alternating and reversing bipolar dynamics between its Yin forms, e.g., dark, cloudy, cold, wet, soft, inner, lower, deep, still, receptive, magnetic, centripetal, receding, contracting, condensing; and its complementary Yang forms, e.g., bright, clear, hot, dry, firm, outer, higher, surface, moving, assertive, dynamic, centrifugal, advancing, expanding, radiating. Yin Ch'i energies are identified with Earth, body, water, night, moon, valleys, ebbing, waning and troughing and the feminine, vulvic and maternal in Nature. Yang Ch'i energies are identified with Heaven, Spirit, mind, fire, day, sun, mountains, flowing, waxing and cresting and the masculine, phallic and paternal in Nature.

SYMBOLIC IMAGE ❖ BREATH/CH'I

Great Tao/Spirit is flowing everywhere, far to the left, far to the right... giving life to all beings. (# 34).

The rhythmic alternating of the respiratory cycle of our human breath vitalizes, sustains and energizes human life. As with breathing, there is a constant, continuous and continual interchanging and exchanging of Yin Ch'i/Yang Ch'i vital energies and life-giving force. The interacting of Yin Ch'i/Yang Ch'i energies generates all of the phenomena of our human existence and experience.

LIVING PROCESS ❖ VITALIZING/HUO

Harmonizing Yin Ch'i/Yang Ch'i energies is bringing all beings to completion. (# 42).

Meditate on the life-giving and sustaining and the rhythmic alternating of our Human Soul's slow, deep and full breathing. Can we harmoniously balance and integrate the many bipolar complementary interchanging phenomena of our human existence and experience?

Transformative Passage 3

HEAVEN TO EARTH/T'IEN TO TI

Tao/Spirit's Heaven-Earth is harmonizing, gently raining down sweet dew which is falling impartially and equally upon all beings. (# 32).

Our Human Soul's passaging from Tao/Spirit's Heaven and Heavenly nature to Tao/Spirit's Earth and Earthly nature is the descending embodying of the nonmaterial and nonphysical energy of Tao/Spirit into the material and physical form of its Tao/Spirit-nature/Virtuosity/Te/Human Soul. The macrocosmic-microcosmic correspondence of Heaven above and Earth below integrates the vast spaciousness and openness of the infinite celestial sky and the solid focused and localized finite terrestrial lands, as expressed in the Hermetic alchemical maxim 'As above, so below' and the theological epiphany of 'Heaven on Earth'.

SYMBOLIC IMAGE ❖ SOIL/T'U

Tao/Spirit's Heaven is protecting and saving us through unconditioned loving. (# 67).

The 'Earthing' of Heaven is embodied in the Valley Spirit of the lush lowlands of Earth that receive, ground and deepen the descending inpouring and inflowing of beneficent and providential Heavenly energies. The Earth's soil is fertile, abundant and luxurious, is nourished by Heaven's loving sunlight and rain and provides the grounding support for our food, life and growth on planet Earth.

LIVING PROCESS ❖ GROUNDING/CHI

Tao/Spirit's Heaven's network is vast and wide-meshed, yet nothing and no one are slipping through. (# 73).

Meditate on being centered between the protective canopy of Heaven and the supportive foundation of Earth; on the valleys, canyons, gorges, caves and grottos that hold its geological records and on its broad rich and friable soil that includes the ground of all planetary life. Can we open to receive the beneficent inflowing of Heavenly energy and allow it to nourish our bodies and grow our Human Souls?

Transformative Passage 4

NOTHING TO DOING/WU TO WEI

Tao/Spirit is constantly not-doing any 'thing', yet nothing is being left undone. (# 37).

Our Human Soul's passaging from the Non-Being and nonmateriality of transcendent Tao/Spirit to the being of its immanent material activities is the sourcing of its own actings, doings and makings in Tao/Spirit and its unplanned, uncontrived, unimplemented and unpurposefully executed activities. The natural flowing of the Wu Wei Ch'i energy of Tao/Spirit is frictionless, effortless and seamless and continuously circulating, coursing and streaming throughout the cosmos and our human bodies, e.g., wind blowing clouds, rain falling to Earth, rivers running along, blood circulating, consciousness streaming.

SYMBOLIC IMAGE ❖ WATER/SHUI

Most Soulfully developed goodness is being like water. Water is benefiting all beings without contending. (# 8).

Pure, fresh and flowing water is a vivid symbol of Tao/Spirit's natural activity of no-'thing' doing that is softening, cleansing, nourishing and replenishing and streaming along without resisting, conflicting or contending with solid objects that are in its way. Similarly, our Human Soul's existence in the space-time continuum, its streaming of consciousness and the sequencing of its activities are phenomena that are occurring naturally unless we interfere with them through planned, controlled, forced and manipulated interventions.

LIVING PROCESS ❖ NOURISHING/YANG

I alone am differing from other people in drawing nourishment from Mother Tao/Spirit. (# 20).

Meditate on activities that are natural, essential, necessary and appropriate and which flow organically and harmoniously from a full awareness of and deep connection with Tao/Spirit's Reality. Can we attune to Tao/Spirit as Source and yield to and follow along with its natural unfolding?

Transformative Passage 5

Spirit to Body/Shen to Shen

As Spirit/Soul-identified Human Beings, we are unifying our Tao/Spirit's Heavenly-Earthly Souls and embodying undivided Oneness. (# 10).

This is the passaging of Heavenly Tao/Spirit into physical incarnation and embodiment where it is incorporated as a body-Spirit, the physical Soul/P'o of Human Beings. Tao/Spirit's Heavenly/Yang Ch'i energy descends at a lowered vibrational frequency and condenses and coalesces into and infuses the physical form of our human body. The embodying of Tao/Spirit's Yang Ch'i energy resides in the lower/belly, middle/heart and upper/head energy centers/elixir fields/Tan T'iens of our human body. Developing our Human Soul involves bringing the Sacredness of Tao/Spirit into the humanness of our body and embodying our Tao-Spirit nature/Virtuosity/Te.

Symbolic Image ❖ Belly/Tu/Fu

Spirit/Soul-identified Human Beings are attending to the belly and not the eyes. (# 12).

It is the lower/belly center that holds the generative energy/Ching that can be transmuted into the vital energy/Ch'i of the heart center and the Spiritual energy/Shen of the head center in the developing of Soul-journeying, Soul-work, Soul-making and the enSouling process. The belly center connects us with the deeply grounding, fundamentally supporting and foundationally stabilizing Earth energies, the humus soil and humble flesh of our humanity and Human Soul.

Living Process ❖ Embodying/T'i

As leaders, when we are embodying Tao/Spirit, all beings are transforming spontaneously. (# 37).

Meditate on opening to receive and transform the descending energy of HeavenlyTao/Spirit and embodying and incorporating it as our Human body-Spirit, our physical Human Soul. Can we lower our human breath and breathe slowly, deeply and fully from our Earth/belly energy center?

Transformative Passage 6

SACRED TO HUMAN BEING/SHENG TO JEN

Most Spiritually/Soulfully developed is identifying as Tao/Spirit's empty inner Center. (# 5).

Our Human Soul is the co-existing integration of an embodied Spirit and an inSpirited body, i.e., both a body-Spirit and a Spirit-body. Our Human Soul is a twin Spiritual Soul/Hun and a physical Soul/P'o. Sacred Human Beings/Sheng Jen have integrated their Heavenly Tao/Spirit and Earthly Tao/Spirit nature, being and twin Souls in the open middle/Heart energy center/elixir field/Tan T'ien of their body; are the mediating link between Heaven-Earth, Sacred Human Being and all Human Beings and personify the Sacredness of ordinary human existence and everyday human experience.

SYMBOLIC IMAGE ❖ HEART/HSIN

Sacred Tao/Spirit/Soul-identified Human Beings are traveling all day without leaving a center of gravity. (# 26).

Sacred Human Beings are Heart-centered, openhearted and whole-heated in their being and living. While our heart-mind/Hsin is more than our anatomical heart, our human heart is a perfect symbol for mediating and centering the reality of our twin Human Souls and the Pivotal Axis of Tao/Spirit and its Earthly and Heavenly nature. Our heart is in the center of our body and its alternating rhythmic systolic-diastolic pulsing pumps and circulates oxygenated, nourishing and sustaining life-blood throughout our body and opens up space for its returning.

LIVING PROCESS ❖ CENTERING/CHUNG

Heaven-Earth's centerspace is like a bellows, empty and inexhaustible. (# 5).

Meditate on our Sacred Heart, the empty open centerspace where Tao/Spirit enters and abides, where our Heavenly Spirit and Earthly body are integrated and where it constantly circulates life-giving and nourishing blood. Can we live our lives openheartedly, softheartedly, warmheartedly and wholeheartedly?

Transformative Passage 7

BODY TO SPIRIT/SHEN TO SHEN

As Spirit/Soul-identified Human Beings, we are unifying our Tao/Spirit's Heavenly-Earthly Souls and embodying undivided Oneness. (# 10).

Tao/Spirit's Earthly Yin Ch'i energy progressively transforms through stages from generative energy/Ching in the lower/belly center to vital energy/Ch'i in the middle/heart center to Spiritual energy/Shen in the upper/head center of our human body. In the transformative enSouling process, our ego 'dies' to Tao/Spirit in much the same way that the caterpillar evolves through orderly stages of cocoon and pupa/chrysalis and finally 'dies' to its emerging imago/winged butterfly. This is the passaging of Earthly Tao/Spirit into its Spiritual inSpiriting where it is animated as a Spirit-body. Tao/Spirit's Yin Ch'i energy ascends at a raised vibrational frequency and radiates and evanesces into and diffuses as the Spiritual nature of our Human Soul.

SYMBOLIC IMAGE ❖ HEAD/T'OU

Without stepping out of doors . . . without looking out of windows, Spirit/Soul-identified Human Beings are comprehending Heaven's Tao/Spirit. (# 47).

It is the upper/head center that holds the Spiritual energy/Shen that has been transformed from the lower/belly and the middle/heart centers in the developing of Soul-journeying, Soul-work, Soul-making and the enSouling process. The head center connects us with the protective canopy, open sky and vast spaciousness of Heaven energies in the clear and open mind of our inner Spirit-nature and Human Soul.

LIVING PROCESS ❖ INSPIRITING/KU

The Soul/Virtuosity/Te of not contending and the potency of not coercing are matching the Ultimacy of Heaven. (# 68).

Meditate on opening to receive and transform the ascending energy of Earthly Tao/Spirit and inSpiriting and animating it as our Human Spirit-body, our Spiritual Human Soul. Can we disidentify from the intimacies of ego, others, world, mind and body and identify with the Ultimacies of Self, Being, Universe, Psyche and Spirit?

Transformative Passage 8

EXPERIENCING TO JOURNEYING/CHING TO HSING

Having the least bit of wisdom, I am traveling Great Pathway, fearing only deviating. (# 53).

The Chinese character 'Ching' in the *Tao Te Ching* is most often translated as 'Classic' but is also defined as 'pass through', 'undergo' and 'experience'. Etymologically, the radical of 'Ching' is 'Mi'/'Ssu'/floss silk that refers to the longitudinal warp of woven fabric and the phonetic for 'Ching' is another 'Ching' that refers to deep flowing underground watercourses. Our Human Soul's passaging from its 'experiencing' to its 'journeying' extends its deeper meaning to Soul-journeying, the conscious Spiritual odyssey, sojourning and pilgrimage of our Human Soul throughout our life-course, life-cycle and life-span as it progresses along the Great Pathway of Tao/Spirit.

SYMBOLIC IMAGE ❖ PATH/LU/T'U

As most Spiritual/Soulful travelers, we are leaving no tracks. (# 27).

Our human living, when considered as the lifelong journeying of our unique Human Soul, is a traveling along the Path of Tao/Spirit which is, in reality, a Pathless Path where those Human Beings who have gone before us have left no tracks. When we traverse the many vicissitudes of our Spiritual adventuring consciously, we are engaging in Soul-work and Soul-making that awaken us to the reality of being an embodied Spirit and an inSpirited body, a Human Soul sharing the blessed gift and precious opportunity of human living with other kindred Human Souls.

LIVING PROCESS ❖ WAYFARING/CHIN

Long Spiritual journeys are starting from first steps. (# 64).

Meditate on our uniquely individual life-course, life-cycle and life-span as the entering, advancing and progressing wayfaring of our Human Soul, constantly transforming from being only ego-identified to being Tao/Spirit-identifying and making the devoted sojourning pilgrimage from the strange land of ego to the Sacred realm of Spirit. Can we forever be a beginner realizing that *being* on the Spiritual Path is the Way-making goal?

Transformative Passage 9

WANDERING TO ACCOMPANYING/YU TO P'EI

As Spirit/Soul-identified Human Beings, we are having no fixed heart-minds and are reflecting the heart-minds of people. (# 49).

There is much to enjoy living a free and relaxed life of 'wandering', i.e., ambling, rambling, roaming, roving, strolling, sauntering, meandering, drifting, etc. without destinations, requirements, agendas, purposes, plans, arrangements, deadlines, etc.. The passaging of our Human Soul from this kind of solo wandering about in our life is one of transforming into a more consciously intended, clearly focused, consistently directed and intimately shared Spiritual wayfaring.

SYMBOLIC IMAGE ❖ UNION/HO

As Spirit/Soul-identified Human Beings, we are bearing the inner shame of our State...enduring the outer misery of our State. (# 78).

There are many Soul-evolving advantages to living life as a unique individual on a solo Mystical path seeking to directly attain a Spiritual union with the Divine/God/Ultimate Reality. Our Soul-evolving is also augmented, intensified, potentiated and catalyzed when made in a unitive relationship with Humanity and with like-hearted Human Beings/Souls who are Spiritual companions; sharing an ongoing deep commitment to being on a Spiritual path, consciously engaging in Soul-work, Soul-making and enSouling and accompanying us on our Soul-journeying.

LIVING PROCESS ❖ IDENTIFYING/T'UNG

Valuing all beings as our true Souls, we can be trusted by all beings. Loving all beings as our true Souls, we can be entrusted with all beings. (#13).

Meditate on Soul-journeying that balances and integrates Spiritual wandering, a solo Mystical path and intimately sharing Spiritual wayfaring with like-hearted Spiritual companions with whom we are united and identified. Can we feel and be one with and identified with other Human Beings as kindred Human Souls on a one and the same Spiritual Path from being ego-identified to being Spirit-identified?

Transformative Passage 10

SELF TO SO/TZU TO JAN

We are having great trouble because we are having a 'self'. If we are having No-Self, we are having no trouble. (# 13).

Our Human Soul's passage from Tao/Spirit's incarnated and personified selfhood to its pure and simple, sheer and utter, and natural and spontaneous presencing is the reality and actuality of its manifesting of-itself-so, by-it-self-so, just-so, as-such, as-is and *as*-itself-so. This is the serendipitous happening of our Human Soul which is unplanned, unrehearsed, unproduced, unperformed and unrepeated. The presencing of our Human Soul constantly, continuously and continually happens naturally, involuntarily and automatically; freely, directly, concretely and immediately; *sui generis, de novo, in vivo* and *in situ* in *impromptu,* improvised and *ad lib* expressions.

SYMBOLIC IMAGE ❖ CHILD/TZU

Embodying abundant Soul, we are resembling an infant child...The natural harmony of the infant child's Soul is being perfect. (# 55).

The infant child and the creative playing of children are perfect embodiments and enactments of the concrete and direct immediacy of the natural forms of our Human Soul's presencing being and spontaneous activities. Wanting to be warm, dry, clean, fed, rested, engaged, close, connected and happy are instinctually-based homeostatic needs that flow naturally from the child's inborn Tao/Spirit-nature, whole being and Human Soul. Anything less, more or other than living and playing Self-So/Tzu Jan is a case of impersonation or mistaken identity.

LIVING PROCESS ❖ PLAYING/WAN

As Spirit/Soul-identified Human Beings, when we are not forcing, people are transforming of themselves so; when we are not controlling, people are regulating of themselves so and when we are not interfering, people are prospering of themselves so. (# 57).

Meditate on the 'playing' of Tao/Spirit in/*as* the '10,000 things' of being, living and experiencing and on the reality that all of our experiences are creative, new and fresh synchronistic and serendipitous happenings. Can we spontaneously live, innocently appreciate and playfully enjoy the Spiritual realities and actualities of being and living our Human Souls?

Transformative Passage 11

EVERYTHING TO BEINGS/WAN TO WU

Profound Soul/Virtuosity/Te is deeply penetrating and far-reaching, returning all beings to Tao/Spirit's Great Accord. (# 65).

Our universe, planet, world, life, awareness and experience comprise an innumerable number of beings, objects and 'things'. This passaging of our Human Soul is from the totality of the '10,000'/Wan to 'this' particular individual 'being'/Wu of the myriad and diverse multiplicity and variety of harmoniously integrated beings. This involves progressively relinquishing and detaching from and reducing and simplifying the number of objects in our external world and the amount of phenomena in our inner world.

SYMBOLIC IMAGE ❖ HOME/CHIA

All beings in our world are coming home to Tao/Spirit like mountain valley streams are flowing into the sea. (# 32).

Tao/Spirit is returning all of the infinite totality of the realities of its originating transcendence to the finite individualities of the actualities of its manifesting immanence within the consciousness, awareness and experience of Spirit/Soul-identified Human Beings. This returning is a Homecoming and full circle from Tao/Spirit's Mystery of originating to the Magnificence of its completing. The returning of Tao/Spirit to its Home of Origin is nothing other than the awakened consciousness of the Spirit/Soul-identified Human Beings who are experiencing it.

LIVING PROCESS ❖ RETURNING/FAN

All beings are flourishing in living, each one returning to Tao/Spirit's Root-Source...Returning to Root-Source is tranquility. (# 16).

Meditate on the endless originating and returning of the birthing, living, growing, declining, dying and rebirthing of our Human Being and Human Souls in the safe refuge and sheltered sanctuary of our native Homeland of Tao/Spirit. Can we experience the Spiritual uni-verse of our Human Soul's re-turning *as* our Sacred, blessed and precious one-turn of Human Life?

Transformative Passage 12

ALL THIS TO AS THIS/I TZ'U TO JU CHE

Here is This, undifferentiated and complete...all-pervading and inexhaustible...I am calling it Tao/Spirit. (# 25).

Tao/Spirit defined as 'All That Is/As It Is/Everywhere/At Once/Here And Now' refers to its totality, actuality, ubiquity, simultaneity, locality and contemporaneity. This is the Ultimate Reality of the Oneness, Wholeness and Completeness of Tao/Spirit that is its consummating, culminating and perfecting within the awakened and identity consciousness of Tao/Spirit-identified Human Beings; Lao Tzu's Sacred/Wise/Sheng Jen, Chuang Tzu's True/Free/Chen Jen and Lieh Tzu's Real/Actual/Shih Jen Human Beings.

SYMBOLIC IMAGE ❖ WHEEL/LUN

Attaining complete emptiness, maintaining constant stillness, we are witnessing all beings coming into being and cyclically returning to Root-Source. (# 16).

The many transformative passages of our Human Soul are reciprocal and cyclical in nature and are our Human Soul's 'round trips' in its wayfaring journeying throughout our human life-course, life-cycle and life-span. The wheel is an apt symbol for our wayfaring Human Soul's endless, continuous and centered circling of birthing, living, growing, declining, dying and rebirthing where its reality is one seamless whole without beginning and ending or where any apparent endings are new beginnings.[14]

LIVING PROCESS ❖ CULMINATING/CHUNG/CH'UAN/CH'ENG

This ancient saying, 'Cycling, being complete'. No idle words. Being complete is re-turning. (# 22).

Meditate on Nature's magnificent cyclical transformings; the Earth's orbiting around the sun, the recurring of seasons, the alternating of day and night, the migrating of creatures and nomadic peoples, the blooming of perennial plants, the reincarnating of Buddhas et al. Can we consciously, freely, freshly and fully live at the dimensionless centerpoint of our Human Soul's circumferenceless circle?

Transformative Passage 13

EGO TO SELF/WO TO CHI

As Spirit-identifying human beings, we are having no ego-interests and are embodying Universal Self. (# 7).

Our Human Souls' passaging from being exclusively ego-identified with body, mind, others and world to being inclusively identifying with/as Spirit, Psyche, Beings and Multiverse is actualizing Soul-work, Soul-making and the enSouling process. Ego is an abstract conceptual image and fictional illusionary figment of socially conditioned fantasies, collectively shared caricatures and consensually agreed upon delusions about Real Selfhood and, as such, requires constant tricking itself into believing and proving that it exists by continually objectifying, construing, defending and asserting itself.

SYMBOLIC IMAGE ❖ LIGHT/KUANG

Perceiving subtleness is illuminating...Utilizing our outer radiating and returning to inner illuminating, we are not endangering living. (# 52).

As shadows and echoes cannot produce the Light of Reality and the Sound of Truth, the derived ego cannot create the substantial existence of a Deeper/Higher Spirit-Self but, in the Light of Spirit and Pure Consciousness, can inwardly realize its true Spirit-nature as the Human Soul from which it originated. The Chinese characters Kuang, Ming and Liang etymologically identify the light and brilliance; clarity and luminosity and radiant and effulgent splendor of the sun and moon and torch-bearing enlightened Spirit-identifying Human Beings.

LIVING PROCESS ❖ AWAKENING/WU

As Spirit-identifying human beings hearing of Tao/Spirit, we are practicing it wholeheartedly. (# 41).

Meditate on the dark, fleeting and fading images and recurrent nightmares and phantoms of being half-awake, dozing, asleep and dreaming that can taunt and haunt our inner Spirit-nature and Human Soul with meaningless, passionless, pointless, fruitless, hopeless and soulless ideas, activities and relationships and distracting amusements and diverting entertainments that can delay, deter and displace our Soul-work, Soul-making and Soul-journeying. Can we disidentify from our personal ego and its physical sensations, mental abstractions, emotional desires, behavioral impulses and relational separations and consciously awaken to the creative illuminated Heaven/Earth-centered and heartfelt Spiritual Reality, Soulful actualities and powerful spoken words and practices of our Deeper/Higher Human Self?

Transformative Passage 14

DEATH TO IMMORTALITY/SSU TO HSIEN

We are coming out at birth and going in at death . . . one out of ten of us is cultivating living very well . . . because within us, there is no place for dying. (# 50).

Our Human Soul's passaging from Tao/Spirit's birth to its ego-death takes place in our consciousness, awareness and experience, since Tao/Spirit is infinite and eternal, unborn and undying. The only birthing and dying of Tao/Spirit occurs whenever it is born, lives, 'dies' or is reborn in/*as* our Human Heart and Soul. So, the birthing and dying of Tao/Spirit is really the Great Passaging of our own birthing and dying as Human Beings, Selves and Souls. Being an immortal Human Being is deeply, fully, constantly, continuously, continually and Soulfully identifying with/*as* that which never was/is born and never will/shall die, i.e., Tao/Spirit.

SYMBOLIC IMAGE ❖ TRANSITION/KUO

If Heaven-Earth is not making events last long, how can we, as Human Beings, be doing so? (#23).

Being born, living, growing, aging and dying are all part of our natural and mortal life course and life cycle. Our Human Soul originated in the Non-Being of Tao/Spirit's Great Mystery and, upon, dying, will return to it; our Physical Soul/P'o descending to Earth and our Spiritual Soul/Hun ascending to Heaven from whence they came into our Human Being. The life-long journeying of our Human Soul is a sojourning pilgrimage from being ego-identified to embodying, personifying, enacting and identifying with/*as* Tao/Spirit for the brief lifetime we have to fulfill and culminate the actualities of our Human Soul and Deeper and Higher Self.

LIVING PROCESS ❖ DESTINING/MING

Continuously, endlessly, the Unnamable is cycling on and returning to No-Thingness. (# 14).

Meditate on the journeying of our Human Soul for the brief, transient, precious and Sacred time that we have on Earth; from the Mysterious originating of its Spiritual Being, to the Miraculous forming of its exquisite edges, to the Marvelous manifesting of its unique individuality and to the Magnificent completing of its radiant beauty and joyful living. Will/can our Human Soul inevitably or intentionally be rebirthed and reincarnated and transition to a new life form and state of being at some other time in some other place? . . .

APPENDIX FIVE
ADDITIONAL PASSAGES

Since our human being, existing and experiencing as Soul-journeying, Soul-work and Soul-making are replete with phenomena and their bipolar complements; there is an unlimited number of transformative passages that can be made and undergone in the life and in the evolving of our Human Soul.

The following ones are some that are mostly psychologically and psychotherapeutically-related and you are invited and encouraged to consider any others that are interesting, meaningful and relevant for you. States and qualities on the left side of each paired passage can be conveyances to transition and transform into their reciprocal complement on the right side and can be opportunities to more consciously integrate both complements.

abuse to dignity	hostility to amicability
addiction to recovery	ignorance to understanding
aggression to assertion	illness to health
agitation to calm	immaturity to maturity
aimlessness to purpose	impotence to potency
alienation to intimacy	impoverishment to wealth
anger to compassion	inability to ability
anxiety to tranquility	inadequacy to adequacy
apathy to excitement	inattenton to attention
arrogance to humility	inauthenticity to authenticity
attachment to detachment	incapability to capability
avoidance to confrontation	incapacity to capacity
blame to accountability	incompetency to competency
boredom to enthusiasm	inconsistency to consistency
chaos to control	indifference to curiosity
closedness to openness	ineptness to proficiency
complexity to simplicity	inferiority to superiority
conflict to resolution	insecurity to security

confusion to clarity

crisis to opportunity

deadness to vitality

defensiveness to receptivity

deficiency to sufficiency

denial to awareness

dependency to independence

depression to happiness

deprivation to fulfillment

despair to hopefulness

disability to ability

disbelief to faith

disclaiming to owning

discomfort to comfort

disharmony to harmony

dishonor to respect

disinterest to interest

disorder to order

dissatisfaction to satisfaction

dissociation to integration

distraction to focus

distress to untroubledness

distrust to trust

disturbance to quiet

domination to equality

doubt to belief

dysfunction to functionality

error to correctness

failure to success

fatigue to energy

fear to courage

fragmentation to wholeness

guilt to responsibility

hatred to love

helplessness to confidence

hopelessness to hopefulness

insensitivity to sensitivity

isolation to affiliation

jealousy to admiration

judgmentalness to impartiality

overwhelm to manageability

pain to relief

passivity to activity

prejudiced to unbiased

problems to solutions

projection to empathy

questions to answers

reactivity to responsivity

regretting to thanking

rejection to acceptance

resentment to gratitude

resistance to willingness

revenge to forgiveness

rigidity to flexibility

separation to relatedness

shame to pride

stress to carefreeness

stuckness to fluidity

submissiveness to equality

suffering to undergoing

symptoms to wake-up calls

tension to relaxation

threat to safety

trauma to healing

uncaring to caring

upset to peacefulness

victimization to empowerment

violation to integrity

weakness to strength

withdrawal to participation

worry to ease

worthlessness to value

NOTES

1. Definitions of the Chinese characters included throughout this rendition of the *Tao Te Ching/Spirit Soul Passages* include their etymological radicals and phonetics and their philosophical extended meanings. Not all of the included Chinese characters occur in the original text and have been selected from reference materials on the basis of their Spiritual relevance for Soul-work, Soul-making, enSouling and Soul-journeying.

2. A typical example is hiking/wandering/roaming in pathless/untraveled/wilderness areas in back/high/open country; where there is not a beverage can, plastic bottle, candy wrapper, chip bag, or cigarette butt to be seen; and being drawn to and suddenly come upon a magnificent natural setting in which to gratefully celebrate the day, peacefully spend an overnight and joyfully greet the new morning.

3. The multiplicity of gods/goddesses, deities and divine beings and divinized, deified and venerated human beings is similar to, but not exactly identical to, the pantheons and hierarchies found in polytheistic world mythologies and religions. And similarly, but not exactly identically, Tao/Spirit as the One Absolute, when anthropomorphized and personified, shares some of the realities, attributes, qualities and meanings of the One God of monotheistic world mythologies and religions.

In the interest of integrating the Divine and the Human, as human beings, we often appear to want our Gods to be human-like and our humans to be God-like. We may do so through the ego-projecting of personalizing God in our image and/or the ego-inflating of personifying ourselves in God's image.

That Tao is essentially a nontheistic and nonpersonal Ultimate Reality circumvents the personalizing tendency of our ego to 'be' or to 'play' God, e.g., to be omnipresent, omniscient and omnipotent. The Tao/Spirit-identified human being does not obtain any 'goodies' by being or playing Tao. Further, in later philosophical Taoism; while some attributes of Tao are originality, vitality and destiny; there is no anthropomorphized notion of a Creator, Supreme organizing and sustaining Being or soteriological Savior.

4. It is important to remember that concluding, completing, consummating and culminating our human experience of living does not necessarily mean becoming a supernatural or superhuman being. The ordinariness of everyday living becomes extraordinarily rare in the instants of awakening to, identifying with/*as* Tao/Spirit and *being* and living as a Human Soul, regardless of how or when it happens.

5. Throughout the Spirit/Soul Commentaries of this rendition, frequent reference is made to 'identifying with/*as* Spirit'. The 'as' *is* a crucial signifier of the nondual and integral identity of human being and Spirit. Human *Being* is being Spirit. This state of identity consciousness is also found in the Spiritual teachings and meditative practices of, e.g., Hinduism wherein Atman is Brahman; Buddhism wherein Samsara is Nirvana, Karma is Dharma; Form is Emptiness, Human Nature is Buddha-Nature and Tathata is Sunyata; Taoism wherein 'the 10,000 things' are Tao and Zen wherein Ordinary Mind is Original/True/One/No Mind and Satori/Awakening is, as Tao-Master Alan Watts put it, 'This is It!'.

Identifying with/*as* Tao/Spirit, our real and true inner Tao/Spirit-nature is identifying with All That Is/As It Is/Everywhere At Once/Here And Now. This is the conclusion, completion, consummation and culmination of human being *as* Tao/Spirit and Tao/Spirit *as* human being; *as* one holographic macroscosmic-microcosmic and nondual and integral identity, our mirror of the Divine and God's window to our world.

6. The Virtuosity of Te is the embodying of Spirit and the Virtuality of Tao is the inSpiriting of body, respectively identifying and constituting our Human Soul as a body-Spirit and Spirit-body.

The Virtuosity of Te/Soul is its existence and actuality and the Virtuality of Tao/Spirit is its essence and potentiality. The Virtuality of Tao/Spirit is not its 'virtual reality', which is only a computer generated cyber-analog of Reality or only a semblance of Reality, e.g., 'She was a virtual goddess but virtually unknown'. Both of which are not real Reality and only approximate it, even with a clear memory and vivid imagination on our parts.

7. Although the totality of the myriad and innumerable beings, things and others and activities, affairs and events of the world, cosmos and universe arguably may have an objective reality and existence independent of human experience; they all are subjective experiential phenomena of our human consciousness and conscious awareness. They also are 'phenomenal' in the sense that all of the Mystery, Miracles, Marvels and Magnifcence of Spirit, our Human Soul and the many passages of our Soul-journeying take place in the Pure, Nondual and Integral Consciousness of awakened and Tao/Spirit-identifed Human Beings.

8. In the questions posed for each of the commentaries on the 81 transformative passages, the use of 'we', as in 'Can we . . . ?', considers we human beings as incarnated Spirit, Human Souls and journeying Souls who are on the life-long wayfaring journeying from being unconsciously and predominantly ego-identified to being consciously Spirit-identifying. Using 'can', as in 'Can we . . . ?', addresses possibilities of enSouling and may, of course, be reframed as affirmations, i.e., As journeying Souls: We *can* . . . ! and/or attainments, i.e., As journeying Souls: We *are* . . . !

9. This is the shortest and most succinct Passage of the *Tao Te Ching*, appears in the middle of the text and is its central and essential teaching at the very heart and core of our human

being, existing, living and experiencing as journeying Human Souls arising from the Non-Being of Tao/Spirit and softening and yielding to the alternating, reversing, flowing and returning Home to it through the natural moving and operating of Yin/Yang Ch'i and Wu Wei Ch'i energies.

10. Actually and holographically, and not just symbolically and metaphorically, Heaven can be experienced as being on/*as* Earth and in/*as* our world. The 'end' of our world may not be some apocalyptic and cataclysmic 'final' event but, rather, may be the cessaton of our exclusive ego-identifying with a separate 'world' and our bringing the 'world' to its natural teleological completion, eschatological fulfillment and culminating absorption in/*as* Spirit, Heaven and the Divine within/*as* our Human Being, Consciousness and Soul.

And, commensurately, the 'last judgment' may not be some ominous and threatening eleventh hour assessment, evaluation and determination of our Soul's fate in a Heaven or a Hell but, rather, may be the final ending of our judgmental mentality and the opening entry into a Heavenly state of pure, undifferentiated, nondual and impartial consciousness; the inner conclusion, completion, consummation and culmination of our Human Soul's journeying back Home to/*as* Spirit, Heaven and the Divine within/*as* our Human Being, Consciousness and Soul.

11. The phrase 'uncondition*ed* love' is used rather than uncondition*al* love. It is virtually impossible to live and to love without conditions and limits, e.g., given the existential facticity of limit or boundary conditions such as being in a body, being situated in space-time, being in a world with other beings and being mortal. Considering the blessed gift and precious opportunity of loving as uncondition*al* sets us human beings up for failing and for feeling bad about ourselves and our ability to love other human beings due to erroneous assessments, evaluations and judgments made in terms of unrealistic condition*ed* standards, collective expectations and ego-models. The term 'uncondition*ed*

love', by way of contrast, suggests a natural human loving that is relatively free of socially conditioned collective, acculturated and conventional fantasies, identifications and experiences of what loving is, should be or could be.

12. And so ends this Spiritual wayfarer's and sojourning pilgrim's rendering of *Lao Tzu's Tao Te Ching*, considered as *Spirit Soul Passages* with Soul-Journeying Commentaries in the form of Meditative Inquiries. Again, if you find this material to be of some, or any, inspiration, encouragement, value, support, assistance, guidance and benefit to you in your own Soul-work, Soul-making and Soul-journeying and your own identifying with/*as* Spirit and its Virtuosity, our inborn Spirit-nature and Human Soul; I am infinitely pleased and eternally grateful. Our Spirit is constantly pure, free and open and our Human Soul is naturally good, kind and gentle!

13. For us in the West, it doesn't take a great leap of faith to associate and identify Great Mother, Mother Tao as Creatrix/Origin/Source, Mother Nature, Mother Earth, the Mysterious Female and Goddess archetypes; the fertility, fecundity and fruitfulness of the pristine, unspoiled and unsullied Feminine Valley Spirit and the natural, virginal and unworked Primordial Simplicity and wholeness of unhewn wood and unspun silk with the sanctified, deified and glorified personifications of the Holy Virgin Mary and the Virgin of Guadalupe in/through/*as* whom conception, pregnancy, human birthing and Motherhood are consecrated, hallowed and given a Spiritual Reality that integrates the inner and outer experience and meaning of the incarnation and embodiment of Divine and Human Being.

14. It is noteworthy that homophones of the Chinese character 'Lun' are constancy, natural relationships, discoursing, winding silk threads, completing, a bundle of documents/bamboo slips tied together, the K'un Lun high mountain range between Tibet and the Gobi and the K'un Lun Mountain of Immortality (The

last known heading and destination of Lao Tzu) which would seem, at least linguistically and definitely metaphorically, to substantiate the legend of Lao Tzu as the purported author of the *Tao Te Ching*.

15. Besides T'ai Chi Ch'uan and Ch'i Kung, the author has found several other moving meditations and enjoyable activities to be of significant transformative value in Soul-work, Soul-making and Soul-journeying, e.g., the physical gesticulations that go along with being Italian and Sicilian; hugging and sharing with family members and friends; playing with grandchildren; petting the cat; watering the plants; cooking at home; hand washing the dishes; strolling on the beach; hiking in the forest; sitting beside a river; walking in the rain; dancing in the full moonlight; singing some favorite 'oldies'; driving on scenic or winding roads; writing or driving to see the people with whom I could communicate via cell phone or e-mail; eating Thai, Indian and Chinese food; frequenting Costco and Trader Joe's for samples; shopping at local markets and stores rather than on-line; engaging and assisting strangers along the way of being in the world; reading Tao books; sending 'Letters' to the Pacific Sun editor; word-play and one-liners; writing down 'expressions' by hand on lined paper; writing books like this one; etc., etc., etc..

GLOSSARY

The following Chinese words are some additional ones not characterized or fully defined in the rendition but which are related to Spirit, Human Soul and their Energies:

Ch'ai — burn bundles of sticks to Heaven.

Ch'ang — gates of Heaven.

Ch'en — the heavenly bodies.

Ch'i — Spirits/Deities of the Earth.

Ch'i — vital energy/life force.

Chiang — descend from Heaven.

Ch'ien — Heaven.

Chin — spirit/energy/vigor/drive.

Ching — generative essence/energy.

Ching Shen — spirit/essence/spirited/vigor.

Ch'iung — an arch/vault/the sky.

Chou — Earth/Universe/infinite time/always.

Chou — spirits used for sacrifices.

Hao — power that rules in the heavens/light of Heaven/God/ clear sky.

Hou — Empress/God of Earth (with Ti).

Hsi — protection/favor of Heaven.

Hsiao — Empyrean/Heavenly paradise/highest Heaven/sky.

Hsiao — mountain sprites.

Hsien — immortals/genii.

Hsin Ling — Soul/Spirit.

Hu — protection/favor/blessing of Heaven.

Hun — Spiritual/Heavenly/Divine Soul.

Hun P'o — Soul/Psyche.

Huo Li — energy/vitality/vigor.

I T'i — one body/Cosmos/Universe/whole of Nature.

K'un Lun — Sacred mountain/abode of immortals.

Li — awe of the gods.

Liang — Heaven-sent gift.

Liang — a sprite.

Liao — sacrifices offered to Heaven.

Ling — offerings to Heaven.

Ling — Spirit/Spiritual/Spiritual power/Spirit of a thing acting on others/Divine force.

Ling Hsin — Spiritual heart-mind.

Ling Hsing — Spiritual nature.

Ling Hun — Spirit/Soul.

Lung — vault of Heaven.

Ming — decree/command/mandate/destiny/will of God.

Nan Shen — male god/deity/divinity.

Neng — energy/capacity/ability.

Nu Shen — female goddess/deity/divinity.

P'o — physical/Earthly/animal Soul.

Shan — Emperor-only made sacrifice to Heaven.

Shang Ti — God/Supreme Being/Lord of Heaven/Heaven.

Shang Ti Shen — Spirit of Heaven-Earth.

Shen — Divine/a God/Deity/Spirit/Soul/Sacred/supernatural.

Shen Hsien — supernatural/celestial being/immortal.

Shen Ling — Spirit.

Sheng — Divine/Holy/Sacred/saintly.

Shih — Heavenly influx/revelation.

Ssu/Szu — faculties of the Soul.

Sui — noxious spirits.

Ta Hsuan — Great Mystery.

Ta Shen — Great Spirit.

Ta Wu — Great Awakening.

Tai — a Sacred mountain.

Tao — canopy of Heaven/sky.

Ti — Ancestor/Creator/Lord of Heaven/God/Supreme Power/Deified Being.

T'iao — offering of flesh to manes/deified spirits.

T'ien — the blue sky.

Wang — a sprite.

Wu — sorcerer(ess) dancing/incanting to induce the descent of spirits.

Wu Hsien — no limit/boundless/Infinite.

Wu Shih — no time/timeless/Eternal.

Yang — Divine judgment.

Yang Sheng — nourish Life.

Yao — five Sacred mountains.

Yao — phantoms/noxious spectres.

Yin — generative force/reproductive power of Heaven-Earth.

Yu — canopy of Heaven/vast space/shelter/cover/Universe.

Yu — Divine care/protection/aid of Heaven.

Yu Chou — Universe/spatial extension/temporal duration.

Yun — life-giving influence of Nature.

Yung Heng — Eternal/constant/everflowing/perpetual/
everlasting/forever/always.

EPILOGUE 1

The following are some images of passages in the wayfaring journeying of our Human Soul from an initial condition of merely existing to a more evolved one of really living. The images also can encourage you, the readers, to create other ones that are interesting, relevant and/or meaningful for you.

From merely existing; eyes closed, asleep and dreaming; in a dark and colorless unbidden world of vague images and surrogate representations; to really living; eyes open, awake and experiencing; in an illuminated and colorful welcomed universe of vivid realities and actual beings.

From merely existing; eyes darkened, a thing and object; in a dehumanized and impersonal materialistic world of anonymous others and heartless ciphers; to really living; eyes bright, a Spirit and Soul; in a human and transpersonal Spiritual dimension of developed Selves, evolved Beings and kindred Souls.

From merely existing; eyes crossed, alone and cold; in an isolated and alienated fragmented world of divided egos and separate others; to really living; eyes focused, uniquely and warmly; in a co-existing and united human community of whole Selves and interrelated Souls.

From merely existing; eyes squinted, afraid and enraged; in an abusive and violent traumatic world of unspeakable invalidation and crippling negation; to really living; eyes smiling, singing and dancing; in a free and vast creative arena of human dignity and self-worth.

From merely existing; eyes clouded, unconscious and unaware; in a strange and senseless enigmatic world of private illusions and collective delusions; to really living; eyes clear, conscious and aware; in a familiar and sensible comprehensible realm of shared meanings and universal truths.

From merely existing; eyes swimming, fascinated and preoccupied; in a distracting and diverting absorbing world of fleeting shadows and fading echoes; to really living; eyes steady, engaged and committed; in a grounded and focused concentrated field of substantial realities and tangible actualities.

From merely existing; eyes glazed, entranced and reeling; in a hypnotic and mesmerizing propagandized world of indoctrinated victims and lost souls; to really living; eyes sparkling, enlightened and illuminated; in a centered and radiant effulgent domain of brilliant Spirit and luminous Souls.

From merely existing; eyes lowered, fumbling and stumbling; in a random and confusing maze-like world of wrong turns and dead ends; to really living; eyes raised, straightforward and surefooted; on a clear and direct guided pathway of right choices and good completions.

From merely existing; eyes trembling, pressured and anxious; in a hurried and frantic survival world of impossible agendas and looming deadlines; to really living; eyes stable, working and contributing; in a supportive and encouraging helpful place of mutual collaboration and equal cooperation.

From merely existing; eyes searching, mired and sinking; in an objectified and hopeless morass-like world of insatiable needs and seductive attractions; to really living; eyes inward, beholding and dwelling; in a blessed and uplifting grateful state of fulfilling experiences and intimate relationships.

From merely existing; eyes teary, discouraged and depressed; in a raw and suffering painful world of dismissed significance and dispassionate relationships; to really living; eyes dry, nourished and valued; in a caring and compassionate loving context of human dignity, great honor and deep respect.

From merely existing; eyes penetrating, pumped and aggressive; in a speeding and accelerating compulsive world of extreme competition and adrenalin rushes; to really living; eyes softened, content and calm; in a relaxed and gentle enjoyable space of pure simplicity and ample sufficiency.

From merely existing; eyes pinned or dilated, high and strung out; in a hooked and wasted addicted world of intolerable withdrawal and habitual using; to really living; eyes natural, joyful and ecstatic; in a sheerly and utterly precious life of endless possibilities and boundless delights.

From merely existing; eyes blind, vacant and starving; in a terrifying and horrifying hell world of disembodied spirits and despirited bodies; to really living; eyes visioning, complete and perfected; in a Divine and Sacred Heavenly paradise of embodied Spirit and inSpirited bodies.

EPILOGUE 2

The Soul-journeying commentaries of this rendition have been expressed in terms of questions and it is fitting that the rendition is concluded with some final questions.

1. a) Whether by the Sacred Mystery of Divine Creation and Intervention or through the profound Miracle of natural selection and evolution and b) given the Marvelous reality of human life and the Magnificent actuality of human being; why, as Spiritual and Soulful human beings, are not more of us stopping, standing still, facing each other, looking into each other's eyes, beholding each other, smiling and laughing, embracing each other, jumping with joy, singing and dancing arm in arm, wholeheartedly delighting in sharing the moment, thoroughly enjoying being together with each other gratefully celebrating the blessed gift of our precious human life and passionately preventing anything from darkening or dampening its Sacred reality, inherent truth, unique embodiment and radiant beauty that, as Human Souls, we all essentially are?

2. If you are a highly developed and evolved intergalactic/interstellar/interplanetary being capable of interdimensional space-time travel throughout the multiverse, would you visit a planet, e.g., Earth, where you are considered to be a threatening 'alien' or would you pass the planet, e.g., Earth, by like our motorists closing the car windows, locking the car doors, looking straight ahead and speeding through a strange, poor, violent or 'bad' urban neighborhood characterized by oppressed and depressed humanoid beings exploiting, violating, abusing, frightening, terrorizing, torturing, fighting, murdering and killing each other?

3. Why aren't we asking questions like: a) Not just is there life after death, but is there life after birth?; b) Not just is there

intelligent life on other planets, but is there intelligent life on planet Earth? and c) Not just are we alone in the vast multiverse, but are we alone in contiguous human relationships?

4. Given the vast number of human beings born over the vast number of years Planet Earth has existed; why have we not by now collectively evolved into a more advanced global community of Human Souls unequivocally dedicated and devoted to safeguarding, cultivating and augmenting the Spiritual Reality, legitimacy, dignity, integrity, viability and identity of human beings and living throughout generations? Why have we not reached or exceeded a sufficiently critical mass of Spiritually awakened and realized elders who, in parenting their children, are intergenerationally modeling and directly transmitting the Spiritual Reality, Soulful actualities, Human truths and Natural beauties of our essential human nature, being, existing and living?

5. Are we still some modern day equivalents of neolithic primates teaching our children updated forms of how to skillfully hunt, what to collectively gather and what to magically worship in order to survive? Are money, wealth, property, status, name, fame and power now the real 'necessities' or indices of effectively and successfully living as a human being or are they some new kind of meat dragged home, made into jerky and salted away for an ego's cold winter? Why does each generation have to keep individually recapitulating and re-inventing the wheel of transforming and developing from identifying with ego to identifying *as* Spirit and Human Soul that it took its previous generations their whole lifetime to complete, if at all?

6. Why, after this long a time, haven't we, as a Human race, awakened to being and living our embodiment as Spirit, our Human Soul and innermost, deepest, centermost, truest and utmost Nature and Being? Once again, why are not more of us walking around humbly appreciating; ecstatically blissed out by; happily jumping with joy over; gratefully honoring,

respecting, cherishing, hallowing and celebrating being blessed with the precious gift of human incarnation, human life and human being and purely and simply sharing the sheer and utter Mystery, Miracle, Marvel and Magnificence of its Reality for the incredibly short transient time and unique fleeting moments that we have together?

7. Why are we instead tragically, soullessly, heartlessly, aggressively and persistently disenfranchising/depersonalizing/dehumanizing/despiriting and/or destroying each other by:

a) Stigmatizing/patronizing/infantalizing/marginalizing/ pathologizing/criminalizing.

b) Devaluing/disregarding/disqualifying/invalidating negating/abandoning/forsaking.

c) Neglecting/abusing/invading/violating/displacing/ usurping/excluding/eliminating.

d) Manipulating/using/exploiting/robbing/cheating/ deceiving/misleading/betraying.

e) Controlling/dominating/oppressing/overpowering/ conquering/subjugating/enslaving.

f) Harassing/threatening/intimidating/antagonizing/ bullying/frightening/terrorizing.

g) Luring/enticing/seducing/soliciting/kidnapping/ trafficking/buying/selling/prostituting/raping.

h) Harming/hurting/wounding/injuring/traumatizing/ crippling/disabling/maiming.

i) Victimizing/torturing/battering/fighting/battling/murdering/killing and slaughtering each other?..... Yes, murdering, killing and slaughtering each other! And why and for what..... food, water and land; safety, sufficiency and security; values, beliefs and ideologies; power, control and domination; prestige, fame and supremacy; freedom, peace and happiness; gold, silver and money; uranium, plutonium and neptunium; guns, missiles and bombs; oil, sex and drugs; 'things', 'toys' and . . . ?

1) While there are many well reasoned and postulated answers to the above questions and many well comprehended and understood explanations, both exoteric and esoteric, as to why our human condition is as it is and 2) While compassionate understanding, acceptance, tolerance and forgiveness may be the most Spiritually awakened, developed and evolved position to adopt with respect to the realities, purposes, functions, needs, limitations, shortcomings and failings of our human nature, being, existence and ego; I have experienced that the questioning of any 'answers', rather than the answering of any questions, has contributed more essentially, openly, truthfully, meaningfully, Spiritually and Soulfully to awakening, discovering, changing, transforming, growing, developing and evolving throughout my sojourning pilgrimage, wayfaring passaging and Soul-journeying during this lifetime.

But, so it is that there *is* one urgent answer to one recurrent question often asked of the young children of our global human world community. As being the Divine bestowals, blessed gifts and precious treasures of Humankind and the Sacred incarnations, embodiments and energies of Spirit and our Human Soul; for too many young children (and one child is too many!), their only answer to the question 'What do you want to be when you grow up?' is 'I want to be alive!'.

CODA

A closing note on our Human Soul's transformative journeying and wayfaring passaging from being a sleeping, dreaming and dying soulless person to being an awakened, conscious and living Soulful Human Being. Our human life course, life cycle and life span are an essential, existential and experiential enSouling process evolving from birthing and soullessly exclusively identifying with body, others, world, mind, ego and dying to Soulfully inclusively identifying *as* Spirit, Beings, Multiverse, Psyche, Self and Living. Being our Human Soul is being an integral embodied/incorporated body-Spirit and an inSpirited/animated Spirit-body, a physical Soul/P'o and a Spiritual Soul/Hun.

As Human Souls, we can undergo and experience passaging from soullessly relating to other Human Beings as separate and isolated egos to Soulfully interrelating with fellow Human Beings as integrated and interconnected Selves who are an embodied Spirit/Body-Spirit and an inSpirited/Spirit-Body, i.e., a Human Soul. This would undoubtedly result in the decreasing of many of the inhumane prejudices and inequalities, contentions and conflicts, abuses and violence, wounding and traumas, battling and killing, disasters and tragedies and pain and suffering that besiege and plague our Human Soul on its wayfaring journeying with kindred Spiritual friends and Soulful companions from being ego-identified to being Spirit-identified.

Some of the nature, qualities, characteristics, attributes and experiences of persons being more soullessly ego-identified and Human Beings being more Soulfully Self-identified are the following:

SOULLESS PERSONS EGO-IDENTIFIED WITH BODY/OTHERS/WORLD/MIND/EGO:	SOULFUL HUMAN BEINGS SELF-IDENTIFIED WITH SPIRIT/BEINGS/MULTIVERSE/PSYCHE/SELF:
Illusionary/fictitious	Real/actual
Separate/dualistic	Interrelated/nondual
Conditioned/dependent	Unconditioned/interdependent
Susceptibility/vulnerability	Immunity/invulnerability
Individuality/particularity	Universality/generality
Multiplicity/diversity	Unity/identity
Mixed/dense/cloudy	Pure/refined/clear
Partiality/variability	Totality/constancy
Bounded/limited	Boundless/limitless
Small/specious	Great/spacious
Brevity/transiency	Longevity/perpetuity
Temporality/spatiality	Eternity/infinity
Personal/interpersonal	Nonpersonal/transpersonal
Secular/mundane	Sacred/numinous
Fatality/mortality	Destiny/immortality
Life-denying/negating	Life-confirming/affirming
Asleep, dreaming and dying =	Awake, aware and living =
The soulless ego's deepest/darkest/coldest/greatest fear and anxiety	The Soulful Self's highest/brightest/warmest/greatest blessing and joy

EnSouling is the ongoing life-long evolutionary process of the transforming/transitioning/transcending of our Human Soul from being totally identified with its illusionary sleeping/dreaming ego-self to its being fully identifying as its real awake/aware Spirit-Self. EnSouling is the integral passaging of our Human Soul:

From its body's physically-based appetites to its Spirit's Sacred incarnations.

From its mind's mentally-based ignorance to its Psyche's awakened illuminations.

From its will's volitionally-based errors to its Nature's intentional destinations.

From its heart's emotionally-based attachments to its Heart's universal compassion.

From its world's environmentally-based influences to its Multiverse's co-habitations.

From its other's socially-based diversions to its Being's cooperative collaborations.

From its ego's fantastically-based apparitions to its Self's substantial manifestations.

From its death's mortally-based finalities to its Life's immortal reincarnations.

> Our Body lives for some time
> Our Soul lives for some lives
> Our Spirit lives forever . . .

Gratitude for the blessed gift of the precious treasure of Human Life and for the splendid opportunity of experiencing a sojourning pilgrimaging from the mental ignorance, emotional attachments, volitional errors and relational separations of a slumbering and fettered ego-based, ego-focused, ego-driven and ego-identified unconscious, profane and quasi-human existing to the wisdom, joys, peace and wholeness of an awakened and liberated Spirit-grounded, Spirit-centered, Spirit-directed and Spirit-identified conscious, Sacred, authentic and loving Human Being and Human Soul.

May you freely and fully enjoy all of the best of good fortune for/in embodying, experiencing, sharing and culminating your life-long Spiritual wayfaring journeying of openness, exploration, discovery, intimacy and fulfillment *as* the absolutely unique Human Soul who you really, truly, deeply, purely, quintessentially and always are.

As Soul-journeying, wayfaring and sojourning Human beings/ Selves; we *can* choose to passage from being predominantly ego-identified to becoming predominantly Spirit-identified Human Souls.

REFERENCES

I am citing only those references and translations of the *Tao Te Ching* made by teachers, mentors and colleagues.

Cleary, Thomas (Trans.). *The Taoist Classics: Vol. One.* Boston: Shambhala Publications, Inc.. 1990.

Feng, Gia-Fu and English, Jane (Trans.). *Lao Tsu: Tao Te Ching.* New York: Vintage Books. 1972.

Watts, Alan and Huang, Al Chung-Liang. *Tao: The Watercourse Way.* New York: Pantheon Books. 1975.

Watts, Alan. *What Is Tao?* Novato, California: New World Library. 2000.

Wu, Yi. *The Book of Lao Tzu: The Tao Te Ching.* San Francisco: Great Learning Publishing Co.. 1989.

All information concerning the Chinese language, characters and their etymological definitions and extended meanings is obtained from the following reference resources:

Dainian, Zhang. *Key Concepts in Chinese Philosophy.* Edmund Ryden (Ed. & Trans.). New Haven: Yale University Press/ Beijing Foreign Languages Press. 2002.

Dong, Li. *Concise Chinese Dictionary: Chinese-English/English-Chinese.* Rutland, Vermont: Tuttle Publishing. 2015.

Fenn, C.H.. *The Five Thousand Dictionary: Chinese-English.* Cambridge: Harvard University Press. 1976.

Fischer-Schreiber, Ingrid. *The Shambhala Dictionary of Taoism.* Werner Wunsche (Trans.). Boston: Shambhala Publications, Inc.. 1996.

Huang, Quanyu; Chen, Tong and Huang, Kuangyan. *McGraw-Hill's Chinese Dictionary and Guide to 20,000 Essential Words.* New York: McGraw-Hill. 2010.

Kluemper, Michael L. and Nadeau, Kit-Yee Yam. *Mandarin Chinese Characters Made Easy*. Rutland, Vermont: Tuttle Publishing. 2016.

Matthews, Alison and Matthews, Laurence. *Learning Chinese Characters*. Rutland, Vermont: Tuttle Publishing. 2007.

Matthews, R.H.. *Matthew's Chinese-English Dictionary*. Cambridge: Harvard University Press. 1943.

McNaughton, William and Ying, Lee. *Reading and Writing Chinese: Traditional Character Edition*. Rutland, Vermont: Tuttle Publishing. 1999.

Star, Johnathan (Trans. & Commentary). *Tao Te Ching; The Definitive Edition*. New York: Jeremy P. Tarcher/Putnam. 2001.

Wieger, L.. *Chinese Characters: Their Origin, Etymology, History, Classification and Signification*. L. Davrout (Trans.). New York: Dover Publications, Inc.. 1965.

Wilder, G.D. and Ingram, J.H.. *Analysis of Chinese Characters*. New York: Dover Publications, Inc.. 1974.

Wong, Eva. Taoism: *An Essential Guide*. Boston: Shambhala Publications, Inc.. 1997.

Wu, Yi. *Chinese Philosophical Terms*. Lanham, Maryland: University Press of America. 1986.

All information concerning English language definitions is obtained from:

Webster's New Collegiate Dictionary. Springfield, Massachusetts: G. & C. Merriam Co.. 1979.

ABOUT THE AUTHOR

Ray Vespe received his B.A. Psychology degree from Cornell University (1958), M.S. Clinical Psychology degree from Case Western Reserve University (1959) and Ph.D. Counseling Psychology degree from the California Institute of Integral Studies (1986). He has educated, trained, supervised, counseled and mentored graduate students in the Integral Counseling Psychology program at CIIS (1972-1990), the Transpersonal Psychology program at the California Institute of Transpersonal Psychology (1977–1979) and the Transpersonal Counseling Psychology program at John F. Kennedy University (1978-1990). Ray has worked in a wide variety of inpatient, outpatient, agency and group treatment settings and was Clinical Director of the Integral Counseling Center (1975-1978/1982-1990), San Leandro Community Counseling (1990-1992) and Marin Treatment Center (1992-2004). He has been a student and practitioner of Tao and numerous Spiritual traditions and disciplines for sixty-three years, has engaged in psychotherapy work for fifty-eight years and has maintained a licensed private counseling practice for forty-five of those years. Ray is currently retired and living in Santa Rosa, California.[15]

www.ingramcontent.com/pod-product-compliance
Lightning Source LLC
Chambersburg PA
CBHW060311030426
42336CB00011B/1001